MARTIN LUTHER—MARTIN LUTHER KING, JR.
AND THE BLACK EXPERIENCE

RALPH REAVIS, SR.

AFRICAN
AMERICAN
PUBLISHING

MARTIN LUTHER–MARTIN LUTHER KING, JR.
AND THE BLACK EXPERIENCE

By Ralph Reavis, Sr.
©1998, 2010 Ralph Reavis Sr.. All rights reserved.

Third Edition

ISBN: 978-0-9817009-7-7 Paperback

Published by:

AFRICAN AMERICAN PUBLISHING
Lynchburg, VA 24501

Cover and Interior Design:
Heather Kirk
www.GraphicsByHeather.com

ACKNOWLEDGEMENTS

The writing of this book puts me in debt to many people. First and foremost are my parents Hallie M. Reavis and Fannie H. Reavis who lived and suffered under the dehumanizing effects of poverty and discrimination in this country.

I pause further to mention the life and thoughts of the German Reformer, Martin Luther, in whose actions I found support for my faith and actions. Yes, I am in debt to all of those from whose lives and writings I have drawn to support my feelings and thoughts. Therefore, whether in the company of a Martin Luther, or fellowship of such persons as Martin Luther King, Jr., J. M. Ellison, Wyatt T. Walker, Virgil A. Wood, Curtis W. Harris, Milton A. Reid, Ralph D. Abernathy, M.C. Allen, H.W. B. Walker, F.P. Lewis, James M. Whitaker, R. Earl Bartley and Jerry Boney, my Systematic Theology professor, we are all a part of the Black Experience in America.

My gratitude must be expressed to Professor Ross Mackenzie who had the capacity to feel with me the pains and the rejoicing of the Black Experience. A word of thanks to the late Miles J. Jones for the conversations we shared about the Black Experience.

Additions commendations are extended to James Coleman, the Ralph Reavis Fellows and learners of the Doctor of Ministry Program, Virginia University of Lynchburg for proofreading the manuscript.

To my wife Marion and family, thank you for sharing the struggle with me.

ENDORSEMENTS

"We are pleased that Dr. Reavis has taken the life of Martin Luther King Jr. and Martin Luther and brought comparisons that help us understand the continuing thread of Christian reformation in the past 500 years. This theological reflection is invaluable in the long journey of reforming our society. This work is instructive and insightful to the journey of African American Christians."

W. Franklin Richardson, Senior Pastor,
Grace Baptist Church, Mt. Vernon, New York

"It was not until I read Ralph Reavis' work that I sensed that Martin Luther's thought and experience had something concrete to say to the Black Experience — Conscientious Christians in every age must slay the heresy dragon of their own time. The Suffering Servant and non-violent approach to socio-economic and political ills tend to produce more Kingdom fruit than coercion; and each new generation of those who would follow the God of faith must genuinely experience God in His righteousness and justice. God's freedom thrust is open ended for all who in faith would enter the Kingdom and work with Him. Martin Luther King, Jr. taught us the same things. White racism is our hersey dragon. The non-violent opposition to it did work and will again if linked to other multiple solutions. This book is very thought-provoking. Read it!"

Latta R. Thomas, Professor of Religion and Dean,
Morris Chapel-Morris College, Sumpter, South Carolina

"There is more than name association in the practical demonstration of faithfulness by Martin Luther of Germany and Martin Luther King Jr. of America, as author Reavis identifies. Both men were God centered and people oriented to the point that both Church and community are the ultimate beneficiaries of their lives. Dr. Reavis' expanded volume links by interpretation two apostles of liberation. The academy and the Church will be the richer for his revision."

Miles J. Jones, Professor of Homiletics, Samuel DeWitt Proctor
School of Theology, Virginia Union Univ., Richmond, Virginia

CONTENTS

FOREWORD

Martin Luther-Martin Luther King, Jr. and the Black Experience by Ralph Reavis, Sr., chronicles the commitment in thought and deed of two reformers—Martin Luther and Martin Luther King, Jr. According to Ross Mackenzie, a former church history professor of the celebrated author of this work, it was the committed character of Luther's mind and heart that first drew Ralph Reavis to the reforming work of the German Monk. Ross further contended that in Luther's commitment to cause, Reavis found strengthening of his own and from Luther's teachings Reavis learned more about his own mission as a black man and pastor. To be sure, the life of Martin Luther has opened the eyes of Ralph Reavis to see what few have seen so clearly—the remarkably suggestive parallel between the first great reformer of the sixteenth century and the black experience of liberation in America.

As it was a commitment in conscious and character to the gospel of Christ that made Martin Luther a reformer unrelenting in his pursuit to look at the structures of his society in regards to Roman Catholic hierarchy, so also was the reformist position of Martin Luther King, Jr. who committed himself to address the walls of segregation and racism. Ralph Reavis who serves as the 16th president of Virginia University of Lynchburg, in Lynchburg, Virginia, lives out the edicts of King's message of the beloved community on a daily basis. Reavis transforms minds with the G.W. Hayes to Martin King inspired principles of self help and interdependence.

AND THE BLACK EXPERIENCE

Therefore, as you read this remarkable analysis of the black experience, please note that there is an observable difference between commitment and interest. Individuals who are interested in noble causes only persist as circumstances permit the absence of conflict and the presence of comfort. Commitment rejects excuses and embraces results that unlock doors turning dreams into reality.

In the aftermath of the historic election of Barack Obama as the first African American President of the United States, I am often approached by individuals of lesser commitment to cause than Martin Luther or Martin Luther King, Jr. suggesting that they are tired and in need of some rest. The only problem with this assertion is that in many instances the individuals have not done any work. You can't take a rest from a rest. The spirit of Martin and Martin models that you have to work before you can rest. This is the challenge of the contemporary Black Experience. Even the church will need to reassert itself to carry on the tenants of Martin Luther and Martin King.

A careful reading of this Reavis masterpiece by those concerned with the continued progress of America as it relates to the struggles of black people will increase awareness of what is required to improve our condition and position in society. Moreover, the reader will gain inspiration to embrace the level of commitment necessary to reform this present age as did the central subjects of this work in theirs. We will forever be in debt to God, Martin Luther, Martin Luther King, Jr., Ralph Reavis, Barack Obama, and one day you for your unconquerable commitment to carry out the truths of this trustworthy text.

James E. Coleman, Jr.
Director, Doctor of Ministry Program
Virginia University of Lynchburg

PREFACE

About fifty years ago in Lynchburg, Virginia, I walked into a newsstand to browse through the paperback books. After looking through some of the books dealing with Greek philosophy, I came to Roland H. Bainton's book about one Martin Luther entitled, Here I Stand. This book gripped me and I purchased it for curious and religious reasons.

I returned to the Hotel Carrol where I was employed as a bellhop each night for eight hours. Those were difficult days for me in my struggle to secure a college education. With the hope of saving my soul I ventured to become a trained minister, clean and upright. That was the stereotyped image of the minister where I grew up. At least, that is what people expected him to be, clean and upright before God and man. This was my goal because my experiences at home, in church, and in the classroom had made me feel filthy and undesirable; in essence, I felt I was a sinner before a God who punishes the wicked. Later, however, I came to an understanding that I could not save myself on my own strength. Luther helped me to realize this understanding. To be a real minster was to be me, uninhibited by any custom or religious tradition without examination.

This kind of experience found a close identity with the experience of Martin Luther as he struggled to win favor with God. The reading of Luther's experience was a benefit to me and a support for my convictions. His struggle with himself and later the Catholic Church at once became an ally

for my personal struggle and the struggle of all black people in the Civil Rights Movements for freedom.

In the early sixties, those black college students who sat in at the segregated lunch counters and went to jail needed a place to stand. They needed some philosophy to give substance and reason to their basic beliefs and actions. At that time, some complacent blacks often attacked us as impulsive misfits who had little understanding of why we were involved in such things as sit-in demonstrations. While all of us were introduced to Thoreau's essay on "Civil Disobedience" before participating in nonviolent resistance, I for one, found more affinity with Martin Luther's stand at the Diet of Worms. I found support in the words of Luther when people questioned me. It was these words of Luther that I repeated to the critics: "I cannot and I will not retract anything, since it is neither safe nor right to go against conscience...May God help me. Amen"*

Fifty years ago in Clarksville, Virginia, I could repeat Luther's statement above to a church which threatened to fire me for civil rights activities for fear of white reprisals. Fifty years ago I could say that to a college president who expelled most of us for our sit-in demonstrations at a segregated lunch counter. Fifty years later, with some degree of understanding of who I am, with some experience and knowledge of the reforming and revolutionary aspects of the Civil Rights Movements of the nineteen sixties, I see more of an abiding affinity of Martin Luther and Martin Luther King, Jr. for the Black Experience.

---

*Martin Luther, Luther at the Diet of Worms, trans. By Roger A. Hornsby, in Luther's Works, ed. By Helmut T. Lehmann, 55 vols. (Philadelphia: Concordia Publishing House and Fortress Press, 1957-69), 32: 112-113.

I

INTRODUCTION

In this chapter the reasons for Martin Luther's experience and the reasons for the black experience are defined, contrasts and comparisons are briefly stated, and the method of approach is set forth.

Experience, according to one dictionary:
(1) implies being affected by what one meets with (pleasant or unpleasant) so that he suffers a change.
(2) knowledge or practical wisdom gained from what one has observed, encountered, or undergone.[1]

Given these two definitions, experience is the by-product of what we meet in life, what we observe, what we encounter, and what we undergo. Human experience is universal; only the conditions under which men live make their experiences similar or different. Truly, all men become a part of what they meet, as Tennyson wrote in *Ulysses*: "I am a part of all that I have met."[2] This is also true of Martin Luther and the black man.

At the outset of this book, it is extremely important that the reasons for Martin Luther's experience and those for the black experience be stated.

It is evident to the writer that there were immediate

reasons and ultimate reasons for Luther's experience. The immediate reasons have to do with the thunderstorm experience and his voluntary decision to accept the Roman Catholic Church's way for his life. As the story goes, in 1505 Luther was on his way back to Erfurt when the sky became overcast. As he neared the village, a bolt of lightning struck him to the ground. In response to this event at the moment, he cried out: "St. Anne help me! I will become a monk."[3] On the basis of this, we can conclude that Luther voluntarily accepted the medieval church's way for his life.

The ultimate reasons for Luther's experience have to do with his whole history. Behind the immediate decision to become a monk lay many factors. However, specifically, his childhood, his education, his father's plans for his life, and the church's way of life were the ultimate reasons for his experience.

A reflection upon his early childhood will reveal how the boy felt about beatings and strict discipline handed him by his parents. In his *Table Talks*, Luther said that his father once spanked him so badly that he fled from him for a long time and was bitter about this treatment.[4] Schwiebert says, however:

But many will recall similar experiences from their own childhood. This was not an age of child psychology, and Luther's parents, like others, lacked the training and time for insight and self-restraint when they felt the moral integrity of their child was endangered.[5]

Yet, it was such experiences which left an abiding influence upon Luther's life. McGiffert observes how he was later to reflect on the discipline of children and their treatment:

With them "the apple ought always to lie beside the rod." And the serious effect upon the character of an over strenuous discipline he depicted in the words, "Where such fears enters a man in childhood, it can hardly be rooted out again as long as he lives. As he once trembled at every word of his father and mother, to the end of his life he was afraid of a rustling leaf."[6]

The discipline in the home and that in the classroom were synonymous experiences for Luther, and they left very little room for him to make decisions of his own. The prescribed way of life was further illustrated in the plans Hans Luther had for his son's future—that he should become a lawyer, marry a rich girl, and, finally, take care of his parents in their old age.

The church also had a prescribed way for Luther, that of steps toward salvation. The grand scheme was all there, offered by the medieval church. It was all laid out for whoever would venture to walk in its way. Luther believed that the only way to survive and be accepted by Christ, the judge, is to do what the church says. These were the ultimate reasons for Luther's experience. Townsend supports these assertions and more:

Luther was driven into the monastery by a combination of forces beyond reason that led him to go against his parents, his friends, and above all, his own better judgment. His accident with the sword, the untimely death of a close friend, and all the formless fears that had appeared sporadically throughout his student days, now crystallized around the thunderstorm event, causing him to abandon the life-direction that had been set for him by his father and to begin in earnest his quest for a gracious God.[7]

It is not until he gets into the monastery and discovers the meaning of justification by faith that Luther becomes a free man breathing a new air.

The immediate reasons for the black experience have to do with men who did not have the freedom of choice as to whether they would accept or reject the life of a slave as their way of existence. This was forced upon them by men who captured them from their families and tribes in Africa against their wills. These men were further reduced to the level of animals and treated as such. Men were considered as things and not as persons. Yet their experience was one saturated with rebellion against such treatment from the very beginning.

Africans drowned in the harbors when they leaped from slave ships and attempted to return to shore, and to escape bondage untold numbers committed suicide during the passage.[8]

Thus, we can deduce that the immediate reasons for the black experience have to do with a people upon whom authority was arbitrarily imposed without their consent.

The ultimate reasons for the black experience have to do with the black man's whole history. Before the black man's coming to the New World lay a long history of exploitation of his homeland by white Europeans and Asians. This in a real way conditioned him for a life of servitude and continued exploitation. It prepared a way for his future destiny in the New World. As Luther's path was laid out for him, so was that of the black man. Du Bois elaborates on this preparation:

Who now were these Negroes on whom the world preyed for five hundred years? In defense of slavery and the slave trade, and for the upbuilding of capitalistic industry and imperialistic colonialism, Africa and the Negro have been read almost out of the bounds of humanity. They lost in modern thought their history and culture. All that was human in Africa was deemed European or Asiatic. Africa was no integral part of the world because the world which raped it had to pretend that it had not harmed a man but a thing.[9]

The rape of Africa long before the discovery of America had established the mood in Europe that the Africans were good servants and laborers. It is no surprise to me that this notion found fertile soil in the descendants of those rapists. The Europeans were eager to supply their counterparts in America with as much human cargo as the Americans could afford. Black men, women, and children were sold as laborers to be worked in the cotton fields and other areas of American enterprises. Both the Europeans and the Americans found the slave trade to be mutually profitable for their economic situations.

By force, then, the blacks' route was clear: they were to

come first as indentured servants and later as slaves to live under an institution unlike any system of slavery the world had ever witnessed before or since. Even the Hebrews in bondage in Egypt were able to maintain their family life and worship their God. These privileges were not accorded to the black man in the initial stages of his life in America. He was reduced to the level of an animal.

The ultimate reasons for the black experience are laid out. The ships were in the African ports to take on their human cargo. And those Africans who were caught for the trip either committed suicide, jumped overboard, were murdered in rebellion, or survived by accepting the ways prescribed for them.

The immediate reasons for Martin Luther's experience and the immediate reasons for the black experience are different in that Luther was not forced by physical coercion to accept the medieval church's way for his life. The black experience will reveal that the black man was taken by force against his will. From the very beginning he protested; he did not accept the life of a slave voluntarily.

The ultimate reasons for both experiences have more relationship than the immediate reasons. Both Luther and the black man, in order to survive, had to follow the ways someone else had prescribed for them. In a real sense, both experiences reflect a condition of slavery with which the writer will attempt to deal. It is to this end that this writer sees meaning for the black experience.

This book, then, is an effort on the part of the writer to look at the meaning of three aspects of Martin Luther's experience in relation to the black experience. At times, the experiences are similar; at other times, the experiences are contrasted.

In the end, the meaning of Martin Luther for the black experience will be determined by what the research reveals.

II

MAN JUSTIFIED

Martin Luther lived a life of struggle to find acceptance before God. He first went through the monastery, but soon discovered that salvation could not be attained this way. The Catholic doctrine of work-righteousness did not bring peace to his soul. After observing the effect of the practice of indulgences upon his nation, he expressed the doctrine of justification by faith and not by works. The Wittenburg tower experience, which revealed to him the meaning of the justice of God, had begun to exert itself. From that hour on, Luther's theme was justification by faith and not justification by works.

This faith could never come from man or the merits of his hands. Luther says, "The Father brings you the Son without the aid of your works and merits. The article of the righteousness of faith is that one believes in Christ. And you have gained the righteousness without works, fasting, prayer, or anything else; it has been given to you from heaven."[1] Faith then becomes a gift from God.

The place of Martin Luther in the theology of the Reformation must seriously be considered with regard to his views on justification by faith. His own thoughts on the doctrine were determinative for succeeding generations who found themselves heirs of his thoughts.

7

MARTIN LUTHER–MARTIN LUTHER KING, JR.
AND THE BLACK EXPERIENCE

There was one word which Luther recalled which stood in his way. That word was in Romans 1:17, and it was the justice of God. Paul had used this word in the Greek language to express a Hebrew thought. Paul used δίκαιος, δικαιοσύνη, and δίκαιος in the letter to the Romans. The writers before Paul, however, had used this term δικαιοσύνη in the LXX as a legal term expressing the sense of "conformity to a standard or norm, . . . conceived of as a norm of human conduct, . . . applied to men and their actions, . . . conforming to that which is required to what is right in relation to others."[2] The Greek word δικαιοσύνη (righteousness) became later known in classical usage, as signifying "the character of δίκαιος (righteous) and that usually in the narrower sense of justice, and the business of a judge."[3] Δικαιόω, in the same sense, means to "render justice," which meant punishment or condemnation. Therefore, like the Greek, the Hebrew standard of righteousness is forensic, therefore, corresponding to the norm of standard which has been set.[4] In the New Testament, however, δίκαιος means:

Clearly a moral forensic term, meaning, in general conforming to the true standard, meeting the ethical requirement under which one is placed. In the main it follows closely the usage of the Septuagint and later Jewish writings, but as applied to men emphasizes even more than the Old Testament conception of divine requirement, fulfillment of which render one acceptable to God, and as applied to God has even more exclusive reference to the righteousness of his dealings with men.[5]

Justice in the legal sense has to do with one standing in the sight of the law. The judge declares him to be acquitted or condemned on the basis of the law. But in the spiritual sense, justice has to do with the standing of one in the light of the law of God. As Paul uses δικαιόω, the word means to make one righteous in spite of the law.[6] To declare righteous or to justify means to treat one as righteous.[7] Hence, as Paul used the term "just" and "righteous," he was setting forth his view of the salvation of man which is given by God. And the

$\delta\iota\kappa\alpha\iota o\sigma\acute{\upsilon}\nu\eta$ $\tau o\hat{\upsilon}$ $\theta\epsilon o\hat{\upsilon}$ (righteousness of God) is the grace of God which saves men from the wrath.[8]

Commenting on this idea of Paul in Romans, Augustine wrote about this righteousness which man needed in order to stand before God. In *The Spirit of the Letter* man could now stand before God because God had manifested his righteousness to him.[9] For Augustine, then, "it was righteousness without merit or Law, . . . but freely by his grace."[10] It was, therefore, the righteousness of God "because God by imparting it makes man righteous."[11] Though Luther differed from Augustine on the meaning of justification in that Augustine held to a gradual transformation of man into the image of God, he was, nevertheless, a great resource to Luther in his understanding of the justice of God.[12]

Yes, it was to Augustine that Luther made reference as he came to an understanding of justification. His lectures on Romans are filled with allusions to Augustine's book, *The Spirit and the Letter*.

This is where he suddenly felt himself gripped by the one word in Romans 1:17, "the justice of God."[13] We can see this struggle in his work in the Psalms. It was here that Luther tells how the fathers before him had interpreted the righteous God. They saw him "to mean that he righteously avenges and punishes, not that he justifies."[14] If God is this kind of a God who punishes and rewards according to one's performance, then who can prove himself to be worthy before a righteous God? This was the essence of Luther's concern. It was his cross until he came to know, after reflection on Paul's Letter to the Romans, what the justice of God meant.

Luther, in his "Preface to Latin Writings" gives an account of this great discovery in the Wittenburg tower:

I had indeed been captivated with an extraordinary ardor for understanding Paul in the Epistle to the Romans. But up till then it was not the cold blood about the heart, but a single word in Chapter 1 (:17), "In it the righteousness of God is revealed," that had stood in my way. For I hated that word "righteousness of God," which, according to the use and custom of all the teachers, I had

9

been taught to understand philosophically regarding the formal or active righteousness, as they called it, with which God is righteous and punishes the unrighteous sinner.

Though I lived as a monk without reproach, I felt that I was a sinner before God with an extremely disturbed conscience. I could not believe that he was placated by my satisfaction. I did not love, yes, I hated the righteous God who punishes sinners, and secretly, if not blasphemously, certainly murmuring greatly, I was angry with God, and said, "As if, indeed, it is not enough, that miserable sinners, eternally lost through original sin, are crushed by every kind of calamity by the law of the decalogue, without having God add pain to pain by the gospel and also by the gospel threatening us with his righteousness and wrath!" Thus I raged with a fierce and troubled conscience. Nevertheless, I beat importunately upon Paul at that place, most ardently desiring to know what St. Paul wanted.

At last, by the mercy of God, meditating day and night, I gave heed to the context of the words, namely, "In it the righteousness of God is revealed, as it is written, 'He who through faith is righteous shall live.'" There I began to understand that the righteousness of God is that by which the righteous lives by a gift of God, namely by faith. And this is the meaning: the righteousness of God is revealed by the gospel, namely, the passive righteousness with which merciful God justified us by faith, as it is written, "He who through faith is righteous shall live." Here I felt that I was altogether born again and had entered paradise itself through open gates.[15]

Here, Luther testifies to the fact that he was a sinner. At first he had sought to gain acceptance before God through the monastic life. He discovered that one could not become righteous by his own merit. To be justified before God comes as an act of grace and mercy on the part of God. The God of wrath became for him a God of mercy. The just would surely live by faith. Thus, the principle of justification by faith was born in his very heart. He had, therefore, seen as Augustine had before him that man received "a righteousness without merit or law but freely by God's grace."[16]

Luther had seen prior to this the Roman church's doctrine of works-righteousness in action. His nation had been

plundered by those who sold indulgences following the command of the pope. This meant that man could, through his own efforts, add charity to faith in becoming righteous before God. To this, Luther raised a question in his *Ninety-Five Theses*. He writes, speaking of the practice of indulgences: "For the graces of indulgences are concerned only with the penalties of sacramental satisfaction established by man."[17] They could not through their own work make man righteous before God. Their work Luther labeled as active righteousness which manifested itself in the actions of men. This, however, would never do. But there is another kind of righteousness imputed to us through our Savior.[18] This type of righteousness we cannot perform but we receive it.[19]

If man, therefore, is a sinner under the Law, it is this man who needs to be reckoned righteous before God, and his being made righteous must come from outside of himself. It must come from God through Jesus Christ. This is the New Testament understanding of righteousness before God. And this is Luther's understanding of justification. We are justified by faith. Luther drives this fact home in a letter he wrote to a troubled and downcast monk in the Augustinian monastery at Memmingen:

Therefore, my dear Friar, learn Christ and him crucified. Learn to praise him and, despairing of yourself, say, "Lord Jesus, you are my righteousness, just as I am your sin. You have taken upon yourself what is mine and have given to me what is yours. You have taken upon yourself what you were not and have given to me what I was not.[20]

He has changed places with us and caused the wrath and mercy of God to be merged together on the cross. Therefore, Luther sees the cross as a means by which God is able to perform his alien work and proper work in the process of justification. The thought is developed in an early sermon on December 21, 1516. Here, Luther writes:

An alien work is his that he may work his own work. His alien

work, however, to make men sinners, unrighteous, liars, miserable, foolish, lost. Not that he actually makes them such himself, but that the pride of men although they are such, will not let them become or be such, so much that God makes use of a greater disturbance, indeed he uses this work solely to show them that they are such, in order that they may become in their own eyes, what they are in God's eyes. Therefore, since he can make just only those who are not just, he is compelled to perform an alien work in order to make them sinners, before he performs his proper work of justification. Thus, he says, "I'll kill and make alive, I wound and I heal." (Deut.32:29)[21]

Justification, then, is the work of God in the cross of Christ. And here we are reckoned righteous before God not by works, but by faith in the act of God for our behalf. In the *Freedom of a Christian* he shows how Christ, through his vicarious death, made us to share in his riches of his grace, which is salvation.[22] For Luther, human works could never have done such a thing. The sinner, therefore, stands righteous before God not because of works of merit, but by faith in Christ.

Luther distinguishes between justification by works and justification by faith. He had observed the practice of works righteousness. "This, however, is work-righteousness, when the papists proposes to do good works before acknowledging the Lord Christ and believing in him."[23] He accuses the Roman church of claiming salvation by virtue of good works, thereby abandoning the article of faith in Christ. They are literally mortal sins without Christ's first justifying us.[24] This is the whole motive of Luther in his *Theses of the Heidelberg Disputations*; to destroy the works of men. Man can never be justified by works; he only adds sin to sin so that he becomes doubly guilty.[25] In answer to Job's inquiry, "How can a man be just before God?" Luther would answer, "A man is truly justified by faith in the sight of God, even if he finds only disgrace before man in his own self."[26]

If man is justified by faith, what relationship do works have to faith? Are they considered in the thought of Luther?

Most assuredly they are. Works grow out of faith. Luther expands this idea in his *Theses Concerning Faith and Law.* But good works come from a person who has already been justified beforehand by faith, just as good fruit comes from a tree which is already good beforehand by nature.[27] This is not meant in the sense that because one does good works he has faith, but rather, the opposite; one does good works because he has faith. For Luther, good works, in order to be good works, must follow justification.[28] This, then, presupposes that God does not accept the works except as he accepts the worker first. Justification of the worker is a prerequisite for determining the value of his works. Luther develops this theme in a sermon on Galatians 1:7. According to Luther, there are two sorts of works. There are works before justification and works after justification. "Therefore, no work can be acceptable to God except the one who worketh it was first accepted by God."[29] The sinner must first be justified before his works are justified.

Luther does not rule out the position of works in that they are good after justification. And yet, at other times, he does not include them. Are we to see his doctrine as ruling out works altogether, that is, as it is found in his *Freedom of a Christian*? Here Luther emphatically states we are justified *sola fide*. We catch his spirit as he says:

Since then, works justify no one, and a man must be righteous before he does a good work. It is very evident that it is faith above which because of the pure mercy of God through Christ and in his word, worthily and sufficiently justifies and saves the person.[30]

In another instance, Luther expounds the position of works in stronger language apart from his doctrine of justification. In his *Commentary on Galatians,* he writes, "that we are justified, not by faith furnished with charity, but by faith only alone."[31]

Are we to believe here that Luther meant to say that justification comes without works of charity and love? In

passages where he stresses the *sola fide* doctrine, this opinion is possible. When Luther reads in Galatians 2:16 that one is justified not by works of the law but by faith alone, he opens himself to exaggeration which later showed itself to be damaging to the church and to the German people. Statements like this can cause problems, as history has shown in Nazi Germany, especially for one who does not look at Luther's theology on the doctrine as a whole. And when this is done, man disregards works and falls into "cheap grace." This misinterpretation of Luther's doctrine in more recent times led the German Christians to be deceived by the Reich. Hitler used the church as a means to his ends. Stewart W. Herman writes:

Many members of the Party, whose faithfulness towards the church was unquestionable, excited in others their own hope that it might become a real movement of the people resuscitating the old piety of the Reformation Period. It was not foreseen that much danger to the church would grow out of the many principles of the Party, especially the racial idea.[32]

Luther placed so much emphasis upon his doctrine of *sola fide* because he mistrusted the Roman church's work-righteousness. In essence, the way of works for Luther was what the church had prescribed for him; and his way of faith was his understanding of God and a relationship with him. It was from this basis that Luther lived and worked the rest of his life.

As this was true for Luther, it is no less true for the black man who was brought to this country to a way prescribed and designed for him. The black man's history reveals this way of works and his way of faith. His history, as previously stated, began with rebellion on the part of the black man in an effort not to become a slave. Records of sea captains reveal how strict precautions had to be taken on board ships with human cargo in order to make the journey across the middle passage bearable both for the slave and for

the captains and crews. Nonetheless, the black man was first brought to the West Indies, Cuba, and other islands where they supplied the work force for harvesting the native crops. Later, when the sugar export received competition from other areas of the world, slavery in the West Indies dropped, a circumstance which made slavery there unprofitable.

Benjamin Quarles observes that as soon as slavery slacked up on the islands, the mainland known as America became the chief exponent of the slave trade.[33] Cotton and other native crops of America demanded the use of slave labor, both for the women and the men.

Plantation-style life became the black man's monastery. Unlike Luther's, however, it was a forced, as well as a pre-scribed, way of life for all black men, whether they desired it or not. Like the monastery for Luther, the plantation system for the black man required that all habits, customs, religion, language, and tradition which one had acquired be given up for a whole new way of life. The plantation, then, became his prison and his bondage, and it was out of life on the planta-tion that his way of works and faith developed.

The way of works for black men was a prescribed way of life on the plantation. It was designed to train black men to be good, obedient slaves. Life for the slave inhibited his op-portunity to live as a free, responsible human being. Ken-neth M. Stampp has observed that:

The only way that Negroes ever learned how to live in America as responsible free men was by experience—by starting to live as free men. The plantation school never accomplished this; its aim was merely to train them to be slaves.[34]

If we accept Stampp's analysis of the institution of slav-ery, we can understand how the slaves were controlled, how they lived, how they related to their masters, and how they expressed themselves. Charles S. Johnson gives us a clear description of the methods used in making a slave suitable for plantation existence:

AND THE BLACK EXPERIENCE

In the early days of the plantation regime, when a gang of fresh Africans were purchased, they were assigned in groups to certain reliable slaves who initiated them into the ways of the plantation. These drivers, as they were called, had the right of issuing minor punishments. They taught the new slaves to speak the broken English which they knew and to do the plantation work which required little skill. . . . At the end of a year, the Master or overseer directed the work of the new Negro who now had become "tamed," assigning him a special task of plantation work along with the other seasoned hands who had long since learned to obey orders, to arise when the conch blew at "day clean," to handle a hoe in listing and banking, to stand still when a white man spoke.[35]

This was generally the pattern of life followed by the slave in the agricultural regions. By and large, he obeyed on the subservient level. However, Quarles suggests that there were other slaves who were treated better than the field hands or the plantation workers. These were known as the plantation domestics, sometimes called the house slaves. They had better food and better clothing, slept in beds, and were allowed more social mobility. Still below them were the skilled craftsmen who received preferential treatment in comparison to the field hands.[36] These were the major divisions of slave life in America.

Given these three different aspects, it is no surprise that the black man could not realize a sense of cohesion on the plantation, though he tried. The separation of slaves into different classes often put them at odds with each other.[37] Coupled with this divide and conquer attitude of the master, enforced upon the slave, was the destruction of his family life. Marriages among slaves did not have to be respected or recognized by white men.

On most plantations, where there was no lack of women, mating ranged from purely physical contacts, often enforced by the masters, to permanent associations, in which genuine sentiment between the spouses and parental affection for children created a real family group. There were masters who, without any regard for the preferences of their slaves, mated their human chattels as they did their stock.[38]

Though in some isolated cases genuine relationships developed between husband and wife, in most cases the stability of a Negro marriage depended upon the disposition of the master. The black woman, like the black man and child, was at the mercy of the master. He could either sell her or keep her. He could cohabit with the woman or he could provide a stud Negro for the reproduction of a stronger stock of slaves. The Negro woman became increasingly important in the same sense that a cow would—to produce additional slaves to be sold for profit.[39]

The Negro woman was used in a variety of ways, which also included being a bed partner for the whites. W. J. Cash observes:

Torn from her tribal restraints and taught an easy complaisance for commercial reasons, she was to be had for the taking. Boys on and about the plantation inevitably learned to use her, and having acquired the habit, often continued it into manhood and even after marriage. For she was natural, and could give herself up to passion in a way impossible to wives inhibited by Puritanical training.[40]

This practice was so rampant that efforts to establish a position against miscegenation were impossible. As a result, Melville J. Herskovits says, "instead of 80 or 85 per cent of the American Negroes being wholly African in descent, only a little over 20 per cent are unmixed, while almost 80 per cent show mixture with white or American Indian, or with both stocks."[41]

Life on the plantation "tended to destroy all social cohesion among the slaves."[42] It destroyed the one institution that was fundamental in any culture for social cohesion, the family unit. The buying and selling of human beings dehumanized the victims. This process was helped along not only by a disrespect by the master for the sanctity of a black marriage but also by a total disregard for the black man's African heritage and culture. In the new environment, the African was forced to give up his language almost entirely. This was done because the master insisted that communication between the slaves be carried on in the English lan-

guage. The master insisted that this was necessary to operate the plantation. In view of this opinion, only a minimal amount of the African language and culture was preserved in the New World. One study holds that "many African words have been preserved in the Negro dialect known as Gullah."[43] This is supported by John Hope Franklin, as far as the language, literature, and religion are concerned.

In the language one can see it in such words as yam, goober, canoe, and banjo. In literature one can observe it in the folk tales that have been preserved in recent years by American writers. In religion there are the divinations and various cult practices, some of which can be traced to the African background. In work, in play, in social organization and aesthetic manifestations there are evidence of Africanisms.[44]

In any event, whatever aspects of African life survived, it was not enough to provide the cohesion that the Negro needed to remove himself from the shackles of slavery. In essence, slavery was his lot and the plantation was the setting for its existence. This institution demanded that the slave give up most, if not all, of his prior culture for a new one. He had no other recourse except to run away, only to be caught later and subjected to harsh punishment by his master, or to rebel, only to have his action, in most cases, end in death. Nat Turner's rebellion and others are excellent examples of this futile attempt to win freedom. They were futile basically because of a lack of cohesion in the black man's environment. For the white slave masters had seen to that by destroying the traditional basis for social cohesion.

His way of works was the life to which he was consigned to live on the plantation under the institution of slavery. He was a laborer to be sold and exploited for what he was worth economically to white folk. This prevailing position of the South pervaded all facets of southern life.

The church and every other institution participated in this prescribed way of life for the slave. Benjamin Quarles holds that the typical way of life for most slaves was influ-

enced "by the psychological and legal controls brought to bear on him."[45]

All slaves were inculcated with the idea that the whites ruled from God and that to question this divine-right-white theory was to incur the wrath of heaven, if not to call for a more immediate sign of displeasure here below. A slave was told that his condition was the fulfillment of the will of the Master on high; catechism for the religious instruction of slaves commonly bore such passages as:

Q. Who gave you a master and a mistress?
A. God gave them to me.
Q. Who says that you must obey them?
A. God says that I must.[46]

Myrdal probably sums up the efforts of the southern systems to justify the institution of slavery best:

Moreover, slavery was justified in a political theory which had intellectual respectability, which was expounded in speeches, articles, and learned treatises by the region's famous statesmen, churchmen and scholars.[47]

Hence, the governor of South Carolina probably spoke the legal sentiment of the South when he said:

In all social systems there must be a class to do the menial duties, to perform the drudgery of life. This is, a class requiring but a low order of intellect and but little skill. Its requisites are vigor, docility, fidelity. Such a class you must have or you would not have that other class which leads progress, civilization, and refinement. It constitutes the very mud-sill of society and of political government; and you might as well attempt to build a house in the air, as to build either the one or the other, except on this mud-sill. Fortunately for the South, she found a race adapted to the purpose of her bond. . . . We use them for our purpose and call them slaves.[48]

A candid examination of the pre-slavery literature in the South, especially the apologetic literature, would give the impression that slaves were happy about their lot.[49] But

there is another side to this impression which is found in the expressions of the black folk.

The other side of the white man's analysis of what the slave felt, thought, and said is what the slave himself felt, thought, and said. Here I am not speaking of what slaves were forced or taught to say with regard to what they believed about God and man. I am suggesting that the black man's way of faith is authenticated by his honest expressions, in spite of the legal, social, and religious confinements under which he had to live. It is in his expressions in the spirituals, the folklore, the sermons, the sayings, and in his efforts to actualize his beliefs that we can begin to understand his way of faith.

A brief offering of these areas of black expressions beginning with the spirituals will substantiate the claim of this writer. The black spiritual is a fusion of the belief and the experience of the slave. It is what he thought of God and what he thought of man. The spiritual is an index into what black folk felt under the drudgery of the controls of black codes. The spirituals speak of life in this world and the hope for a better world to come. They speak of slavery and the desire to be free. The themes of these songs are full of descriptions from the Hebrew-Christian Bible. The spirituals then are interpretations of what black folk felt about who God was and who they were.

Scholars have argued the origins of these songs in two ways. The spiritual is either the by-product of the white religious revival meetings, or it is the Negroes' unique creation. However, I tend to agree with James Weldon Johnson:

The Spirituals are purely and solely the creation of the American Negro; that is, as much as any music can be the pure and sole creation of any particular group. As their production, although seemingly miraculous, can be accounted for naturally. The Negro brought with him from Africa his native musical instinct and talent, and that was no small endowment to begin with.[50]

The spiritual is only related to the white man's religion

in that it uses the language, meaning the English language which the slave was taught. As has been stated, the slave was not allowed to speak his native tongue for fear of the master's inability to control him. Another reason for forbidding him to communicate in his native language was the master's fear of his plotting for rebellion. Therefore, the master insisted on the slaves' learning the English language.

One collector shares the origin of the spiritual in the words of a slave. Here the slave tells the collector how a song is made:

I'll tell you, it's dis way. My master call me up and order me a short peck of corn and a hundred lash. My friend see it, and is sorry for me. When dey come to de praise-meeting dat night dey sing about it. Some's very good singers and know how; and dey work it in—work it in, you know, till they get it right; and dat's the way.[51]

If we can trust this slave's testimony, it is conceivable to say that it is no strain on the imagination to see in the spirituals the originality of a Negro creation. For in them we see the slaves' trials paralleling those of the Israelites in Egypt. The pharaoh of Egypt was his master on the plantation. The oppressors in Egypt were the oppressors on the plantation. The slaves were able to see the similarity between the two personalities. The one in the Bible and the one whom he knew too well. It is no wonder "Go Down Moses" was a forbidden song on the plantation. Harriet Tubman, known to blacks as their Moses for her work in the Underground Railroad, has told us so.[52] In spite of the restrictions, the slaves kept on singing the spiritual.

The notion among whites that the slaves never contemplated their low estate here but rather sang about another land, is stretching the point. While the latter is a half-truth, it is also true that the slave songs reflect both a wish for a better abode, and, more important, a protest against the social ills under which the slave suffers. Benjamin E. Mays punctuates this way of faith:

Although the majority of the Spirituals are compensatory and other-worldly, it would be far from the truth to say that all of them are of that character. Even in the Spirituals the Negro did not accept without protest the social ills which he suffered. "Go Down, Moses," "Oh, Freedom," and "No More, No More, No More Auction Block For Me" are illustrative of the Spirituals that revolt against earthly conditions without seeking relief in Heaven. It seems that the Negro was accustomed to interpret Negro slavery in terms of Egyptian bondage. Throughout such interpretations, he implied that as freedom came to the Hebrews it would come to the Negro. The approach is subtle. "When Israel was in Egypt's land, Let my people go; Oppressed so hard they could not stand, Let my people go; Go down, Moses, way down in Egypt's land; tell ole pharaoh— Let my people go." "Oh, Freedom!" is more militant. It shows that the Negro was determined to be a free people. . . . "be-fo' I'd be a slave, I'd be buried in my grave, an' go home to my Lord an' be free."[53]

Yes, while whites poked fun at the way the slaves sang, little did they know that the same slave would cut throats. That same slave was expressing contempt for the way he was being treated. Wherever slavery has existed, whether in ancient or modern times, it has been resisted. And slavery in America was no exception. John Hope Franklin tells us that the slaves developed a unique way of misleading their masters as to the real thoughts of their minds and souls:

Their work songs and spirituals, regarded by the masters as beautiful expressions of longing for another world, were often expressions of outrage and contempt. "Ev'rybody talking 'bout heaven ain't going there" and "Let my people go" were satisfying both to Master and slave for entirely different reasons.[54]

The slave who sang this kind of music could hold secret meetings to plan a rebellion, solidify his intentions to run away on the Underground Railroad, or soothe his rage. This technique of communication was used effectively as the newspaper or television or radio is used today to get the word around about what is coming up. These secret meetings

were used for the purposes of planning strategy to deal with the oppressor. Frederick Douglass makes reference to the double talk of the slave song:

A keen observer might have detected in our repeated singing of

> O Canaan, sweet Canaan,
> I am bound for the land of Canaan,

something more than a hope of reaching heaven. We meant to reach the North, and the North was our Canaan.

> I thought I heard them say
> There were lions in the way;
> I don't expect to stay
>   Much longer here.
> Run to Jesus, shun the danger.
>   I don't expect to stay
>   Much longer here,

was a favorite air, and had a double meaning. On the lips of some it meant the expectation of a speedy summons to a world of spirits, but on the lips of our company it simply meant a speedy pilgrimage to a free state, and deliverance from all the evils and dangers of slavery.[55]

From these examples of the spirituals, we can see that the songs depicted the spirit of a people who not only reluctantly adjusted to slavery, but also a people who longed for liberation and sought it vigorously. Miles Mark Fisher contends that some of the songs were products of the most militant slaves. For example, "Steal Away" is attributed to Nat Turner.[56] To hear the words of this moving song would lead one to feel Nat Turner's awareness of his impending doom. As he met with his companions in the woods of Southampton County, Virginia, plotting and planning, it is not difficult to conclude that he did not have long to stay here. Meditating on the vision that he saw, it is not difficult for

one to hear, as he must have heard, the "Lawd" calling him by the thunder and the lightning and the trumpet sounding within his soul—he didn't have long to stay here.

An account of Nat Turner's vision is evidence of his awareness and inner struggle to work out a functional theology of liberation, a basis for his actions:

And about this time I had a vision—and I saw white spirits and black spirits engaged in battle, and the sun was darkened—the thunder rolled in the Heavens, and blood flowed in streams—and I heard a voice saying, "Such is your luck, such you are called to see, and let it come rough or smooth, you must surely bare it." I now withdrew myself as much as my situation would permit, from the intercourse of my fellow servants, for the avowed purpose of serving the spirit more fully—and it appeared to me, and reminded me of the things it had already shown me, and it would then reveal to me the knowledge of the elements, the revolution of the planets, the operation of tides, the changes of the seasons.[57]

In those days a self-determining black man did not have long to stay here. There was no place for him as there is no place for him now. The only difference now is that if he becomes a part of the very structures of evil which oppress people he can stay here longer than Nat Turner. I am sure history has shown that those slaves who obeyed were rewarded with a longer physical life. Even though that life was one governed by laws, religious and legal restrictions, which they had no participation in shaping. Nat Turner, however, as Denmark Vesey had done before, attempted to interpret the scriptures and work out a functional theology to apply to the actions which he was sure to take.

Nat Turner was probably one of the best interpreters of the Bible we had in the slavery era. He not only interpreted the scriptures for himself and his black brothers, but he did it independently of the white church. As has been stated, the white church could not have had anything whatsoever to do with Nat Turner's faith. This is based on the examples of its liturgy taught to the slaves and also what ex-slaves had to

say about it. One ex-slave preacher tells how his master told him to preach to the niggers and what he himself actually did beyond that:

I been preaching the gospel and farming since slavery time. I jined the church 'most 83 years ago when I was Major Guads' slave, and they baptized me in the spring branch close to where I finds the Lord. When I starts preaching I couldn't read or write and had to preach what Master told me, and he say tell them niggers iffen they obeys the Master they goes to Heaven; but I knowed there's something better for them, but daren't tell them 'cept on the sly. That I done lots. I tells 'em iffen they keeps praying the Lord will set 'em free.[58]

The knowledge and desire of something better for his people as practiced by this slave preacher is further evidence of what the black man's faith is all about. His faith is not about the desire to remain a burden bearer; but it is faith that points beyond the life he now must live. It is a faith which longs for freedom from the shackles of slavery. It is a faith which provides for a basis of action, even if that action meant lying to his white master. As this slave'preacher acted, so did Nat Turner. His example is a clear illustration of how some slaves manifested in their being what they thought in their minds and felt in their hearts. Nat Turner not only talked but planned and executed his plan to its logical conclusion. He actualized his faith by killing the oppressor and over fifty more along the way. His plan, however, failed because of a lack of discipline to combat on the part of other slaves, a lack of cohesion in the Negro family life, and some slaves' acceptance of the white man's concepts of the Christian faith. All slaves did not do their own interpreting of the Bible as did Nat Turner; the whites had done it for them.

Nat Turner's rebellion and defiance resounded through the sermons and sayings of blacks throughout the slave era and beyond it. In an address entitled "To Those Who Keep Slaves and Approve the Practice," Richard Allen, who

founded the first black Methodist Church in America, spoke of his disdain for slavery and his belief that God was an ally in the slave's cause:

When you are pleaded with, do not you reply as Pharaoh did, "Wherefore do ye, Moses and Aaron, let the people from their work, behold the people of the land now are many, and you make them rest from their burden." We wish you to consider that God himself was the first pleader of the cause of slaves. . . . "If you love your children, if you love your country, if you love the God of love, clean your hands from slaves."[59]

A more forceful approach than that of Allen comes from the lips of the Reverend Henry Highland Garnet in "An Address to the Slaves of the United States of America." Here he sets forth the belief that God approves of the fight for freedom. The words are in the tradition of Nat Turner:

If a band of heathen men should attempt to enslave a race of Christians, and to place their children under the influence of some false religion, surely Heaven would frown upon the men who would not resist such aggression, even to death. If, on the other hand, a band of Christians should attempt to enslave a race of heathen men, and to entail slavery upon them, and to keep them in heathenism in the midst of Christianity, the God of heaven would smile upon every effort which the injured might make to disenthrall themselves.

Brethren, it is wrong for your lordly oppressors to keep you in slavery as it was for the man thief to steal our ancestors from the coast of Africa. You should therefore now use the same manner of resistance as would have been just in our ancestors when the bloody footprints of the first remorseless soul-thief was placed upon the shores of our fatherland. The humblest peasant is as free in the sight of God as the proudest monarch that ever swayed a sceptre. Liberty is a spirit sent out from God and, like its great Author, is no respecter of persons.

Brethren, the time has come when you must act for yourselves. It is an old and true saying that, "if hereditary bondsmen would be free, they must themselves strike the blow."[60]

The black man who could think for himself always called into question the contradictions in the white man's religion. He always felt that God bitterly opposed the practice of slavery even to the point of approving an uprising or violent rebellion. Yet, his sayings reflect also the passionate pleading to the white man's conscience to recognize his wrong deeds. There is almost always this mixture, with few exceptions, of violent opposition to slavery and the willingness to give the white man a chance to mend his ways. This idea is put forth in the words of Gustavus Vassa, the African who was kidnapped and brought to this country to a plantation in Virginia. He tells of what he saw on board the ship. He combines the condemnation of the practice of slavery with a call to the conscience of the white nominal Christian to look at what he is doing to the black man in light of the Christian faith.

I remember in the vessel in which I was brought over, in the men's apartment, there were several brothers who, in the sale, were sold in different lots, and it was very moving on this occasion to see and hear their cries at parting. O ye nominal Christians; might not an African ask you; "Learned you this from your God, who says unto you, 'Do unto all men as you would men should do unto you'? Is it not enough that we are torn from our country and friends, to toil for your luxury and lust of gain? Must every tender feeling be likewise sacrificed to your avarice? . . . Surely this is a new refinement in cruelty which, while it has no advantage to atone for it, this aggravates distress and adds fresh horrors even to the wretchedness of slavery."[61]

Gustavus Vassa, further holds that God never intended one man should have control over another. This was for him a violation of the natural right of mankind.[62]

Another voice heard in the days of slavery not only affirms the black man's struggle against slavery, but also his appreciation to God for the color of his skin. David Walker is not ashamed of the blackness which his creator has given to

the Negro. He does not appreciate those whites who say that it is unfortunate that we were made black. He speaks of them with disrepute:

They think because they hold us in their infernal chains of slavery, that we wish to be white, or of their color—but they are dreadfully deceived—we wish to be just as it pleased our Creator to have us and no avaricious and unmerciful wretches, have any business to make slaves of, or hold us in slavery. How would they like for us to make slaves of, and hold them in cruel slavery, and murder them as they do us?—But is Mr. Jefferson's assertion true? Viz. "that it is unfortunate for us that our Creator has been pleased to make us black." We will not take his say so, for the fact.[63]

This position is important because it documents the affirmation of black people during slavery of their worth in the sight of God. Though for many, blackness was something to be ashamed of, for others who felt all right about themselves, blackness was a gift of God. And this self-affirmation and self-awareness under God was not to be given up in pursuit of whiteness. Lerone Bennett, tells of one Samuel Ringgold Ward, who vowed that he would rather go to hell black than go to heaven white.

"My friends," he says, "hear me for my cause and be silent that you may hear me. . . . I have often been called a nigger, and some have tried to make me believe it; and the only consolation that has been offered me for being called nigger was that when I die and go to heaven, I shall be white. But if I cannot go to heaven as black as God made me, let me go down to hell and dwell with the Devil forever."[64]

This kind of affirmation has no possible connection with the imitation of white society as a residual mannerism from the "house slave." Nor is it the view of what E. Franklin Frazier calls the rising middle-class Negro's world of make-believe.[65] This is the affirmation of a black man who imitates no one but takes his chances with who he is, even if it means hell.

Self-affirmation also appears in the thought of Frederick Douglass. Douglass was born a slave in Maryland and, up to the time of Booker T. Washington, he was the most outspoken voice of the Negro against slavery. He was an abolitionist to the very core of his being. His experience as a slave caused him to wonder about the justice of God. He often wondered why and how God chose to make some slaves and others masters. Douglass knew something was wrong with this kind of system. In his efforts to find out what was wrong, he developed a revealing position on the state of religion in the United States. Here he criticizes the role of the church in the maintenance of slavery:

But the church of this country is not only indifferent to the wrongs of the slave, it actually takes sides with the oppressors. It has made itself a bulwark of American slavery, and the shield of American slave-hunters. Many of its most eloquent Divines, who stand as the very light of the church, have shamelessly given the sanction of religion and the Bible to the whole slave system. They have taught that man may, properly, be a slave; that the relation of master and slave is ordained of God; that to send back an escaped bondman to his master is clearly the duty of all followers of the Lord Jesus Christ; and this horrible blasphemy is palmed off upon the world of Chritianity.[66]

Here Douglass affirms God as the father of all men and attempts to draw upon that fact to effect social change in this world. Douglass is under no illusions about the role of the white church in maintaining slavery and its tacit approval of laws governing his black counterparts. For him, God is not partial in his dealings with men. If there is any fault in the way things are, in the human affairs of mankind, it is man's fault and not God's. Douglass saw the needs of man in this world and would have nothing to do with a God that did not in some way provide for those needs. The prominent idea here is that God did not ordain slavery as was being taught by the churches in the United States.

The sayings of the period prior to the Civil War and after follow both an accommodation way of faith and a way of

faith which defies adjustment to slavery. But I have chosen primarily to use those sayings which defy the white man's prescribed way of life for the slave. I have done this because I believe that the black man's way of faith is found in those sayings which are developed independently or in spite of white oppression.

One may observe this in the writings of Frederick Douglass as opposed to those of Jupiter Hammon and Phillis Wheatley. Although Phillis Wheatley wakes up to some awareness about who she is, it is rather late in her life when she discovers what the whites have done to her. The young Phillis writes:

> Twas mercy brought me from my Pagan land,
> Taught my benighted soul to understand
> That there's a God, that there's a Savior too;
> Once I redemption neither sought nor knew.
> Some view our sable race with scornful eye,
> "Their color is a diabolic die."
> Remember, Christians, Negroes, black as Cain,
> May be refined, and join th' angelic train.[67]

One can see and hear the white religious trimmings in the young Phillis who has some awareness of who she is and what the slavery actually did to her. We hear a deep sorrowful heart.

> Should you, my lord, while you pursue my song
> Wonder from whence my love of Freedom sprung,
> Whence flow these wishes for the common good,
> By feeling hearts alone best understood,
> I, young in life, by seeming cruel fate
> Was snatch'd from Africa's fancy'd happy seat:
> What pangs excruciating must molest,
> What sorrows labour in my parent's breast?
> Steel'd was the soul and by no misery mov'd
> That from a father seiz'd his babe belov'd
> Such, such my case. And can I then but pray
> Others may never feel tyrannic sway?[68]

It is obvious that the early writings of Wheatley and all those of Jupiter Hammon were influenced by the benevolence of the white masters. In most instances where a Negro is treated better by whites, whether it is paternalism or pseudo-philanthropy, that Negro's utterances are less critical of what whites are doing to other blacks. This is true of Booker T. Washington as opposed to W. E. B. Du Bois or Marcus Garvey. The tension is always there between these two types of Negroes. Though Du Bois and Garvey stayed at each other's throats, they were together on the dignity of black men. Two utterances of Washington's and Du Bois's response, are sufficient to point up this tension. "In all things that are purely social we can be as separate as the fingers, yet one as the hand in all things essential to mutual progress."[69] To this, Du Bois responds:

This "Atlanta Compromise" is by all odds the most notable thing in Mr. Washington's career. The South interpreted it in different ways; the radicals received it as a complete surrender of the demand for civil and political equality; the conservatives, as generously conceived working basis for mutual understanding.... And yet the time is come when one may speak in all sincerity and courtesy of the mistakes and shortcomings of Mr. Washington's career, as well as of his triumphs, without being thought captious or envious, and without forgetting that it is easier to do ill than well in the world.[70]

Du Bois's response to Washington is understandable when we observe the accommodative role and concessions that he made in order to keep friendship and receive money to foster his programs. At one point, Washington even agreed with some whites who held that slavery was necessary to prepare the Negro for freedom. He perceives slavery as ordained by God. "God for two hundred and fifty years, in my opinion, prepared the way for the redemption of the Negro through industrial development."[71] It is clear that Booker T. Washington is speaking out of the context of his desire to maintain a pleasant relationship with white people

at the expense of affirming the whole God-given dignity and worth of the Negro, right now. For Washington, the total freedom, political and other freedoms, must be postponed, must be merited through hard work. In other words, the Negro had to prove to the white man that he was loyal and respectable. His freedom must wait until he learned to work industriously and developed patience.

Du Bois, however, offers a more modern conception of the worth and dignity of the black man, and all men for that matter. There is a universal ring in his thought. He expressed this in his *Credo*:

I believe in God, who made of one blood all nations that on earth do dwell. I believe that all men, black, brown and white, are brothers, varying through time and opportunity, in form and gift and feature, but differing in no essential particular, and alike in soul and the possibility of infinite development.

Especially do I believe in the Negro Race; in the beauty of its genius, the sweetness of its soul, and its strength in that meekness which shall yet inherit this turbulent earth. . . .

I believe in the Prince of Peace. I believe that War is Murder. I believe that armies and navies are at bottom the tinsel and braggadocio of oppression and wrong, and I believe that the wicked conquest of weaker and darker nations by nations whiter and stronger but foreshadows the death of that strength.

I believe in Liberty for all men; the space to stretch their arms and their souls, the right to breathe and the right to vote, the freedom to choose their friends, enjoy the sunshine, and ride on the railroads uncursed by color; thinking, dreaming, working as they will in a kingdom of beauty and love.[72]

Howard Thurman supports Du Bois's contention that all men are brothers, and speaks of that instrument which can bring about such a community on earth. For Thurman, that instrument is the Christian ethic of love in the hands of oppressed and oppressor alike. He identifies Jesus as a member of the oppressed group of his day and tells how Jesus dealt with the situation. There is a message for the Negro in the life-style of Jesus. There is a message for the Negro in the philosophy of Jesus.

Living in a climate of deep insecurity, Jesus, faced with so narrow a margin of civil guarantees, had to find some new basis upon which to establish his sense of well-being. He felt that the goals of religion as he understood them could never be worked out within the then-established order. Deep from within that order he projected his dream, the logic of which would give to all—Jew and Gentile—the needful security. There would be room for all: and no man would be a threat to his brother. "The Kingdom of God is within." "The Spirit of the Lord is upon me because he hath anointed me to preach the gospel to the poor.". . .

The basic fact seems to be clear to me that Christianity as it was born in the mind of Jesus appears as a technique of survival for the oppressed.[73]

Thurman saw in the technique of nonviolence, based on the Christian ethic of love, a useful instrument to bring about the kind of community where all is not an end in itself. For beyond the segregated lunch counters and other civil restrictions imposed upon Negroes lay the ultimate purpose of bringing men together. Beyond the white man's hate for the disinherited poor lay the ultimate purpose of God's desire to bring men together in community. "Love creates community. In this sense love becomes the precious ingredient that makes for the survival of the brothers, black and white."[74] Thurman believes love can do its work if given a chance by men.

The black man has a way of faith, a faith born out of struggle. His faith is found in his effort to express himself in spite of the social, religious, and legal restrictions under which he lives. Whether this faith is expressed in the spiritual, the folklore, the sermon, or the saying, or the effort to actualize his faith, it is in his religion that we see his faith. It is in what he believes about himself and what he believes about God that we see his faith. It is in how he used his faith to deal with the oppressor and to adjust to his own psychological needs that we understand his way of faith. As Larry Moore, Jr., observes:

Moreover, in the recesses of his soul and in the company of his brother believers he experienced an existential freedom crucial to his identity and not subject to the bonds of masters; the black man

could be free in the sense of being at one with himself, and in his church this freedom was shared.[75]

This is true today as he views the subtle but deep-seated structures of racism which keep him from full freedom and participation in the whole life of the nation. Looking at such awesome and overpowering forms of evil, the black man has had to rely on his faith to carry him through. The faith born out of suffering in the slave experience and the years following emancipation have helped the black man find a sense of community. It not only has provided this sense of community, but it has offered him an undying hope in the future.

This faith has also enabled him to stand up under the pressures of an unjust society and has often inspired him to challenge those structures which are contrary to the American ideals inherent in the Bill of Rights and the Constitution. What Richard Wright said long ago still holds true for the most of us blacks:

We are crossing the line you dared us to cross, though we pay in the coin of death! The seasons of the plantation no longer dictate the lives of many of us; hundreds of thousands of us are moving into the sphere of conscious history.[76]

As Martin Luther discovered himself and the gospel in a monastery, the black man is now beginning to understand what his monastery, the plantation, did to him. He is discovering and affirming himself; he is no longer ashamed. All that was taken from him on the plantation has inspired him to reclaim it. And he does not need to prove to the white man through work that he is all right. He now knows that he is all right in the sight of God and man. He is recognizing the contradictions in Western culture and his worth, with an increasing appreciation for his own obscured culture. The black man is taking from the culture of the slave experience those ideas and the personalities who fostered them; in spite of the white man's domination, he is using them as a basis for developing new techniques for struggle. He feels a freedom now as never before to reach beyond his abode of confinement in the United States to join hands with his other peoples of the world and their philosophies. Armed with his own experience, faith, and this broader field of knowledge, he is beginning to hold America up and look at her structures as an X-ray machine sees the innermost parts of the human body.

III

MAN IN SOCIETY

In the previous chapter, I have attempted to state the formulation of Martin Luther's thought and that of the black man. These two areas of thought are placed in two contexts, the first being the way of works and the second being the way of faith. An attempt is made to show how each developed. In this chapter; however, I shall explore the comparative and divergent paths these two areas took as to their manifestations. When I speak of paths, I am speaking of two roles; one of a reformer and the other of a revolutionary.

In other words, how does one label a person or persons who have developed a particular point of view or ideology? In what tradition does he or do they stand? To answer these questions, I have chosen to look at the writings of Martin Luther, Muentzer, Martin Luther King, Jr., and the Panthers, with some allusions to other black groups only to point up the differences or similarities.

A reformer, as we shall see, is one who does not attempt to overthrow the existing order, whether it be religious or civil. A reformer merely attempts to revise or purify what already is on the basis of some original pattern. Surely, this was the case in the approach of Martin Luther. As Jaroslav Pelikan observes:

Luther's reformation was a crisis of the very structures in which he

himself, as a man and a Christian and a priest, was fundamentally and personally involved: the ordained priesthood, monasticism, the practice of infant baptism, the canon law, and sacramental system.[1]

This being the case, Luther was concerned primarily with reforming the structures of the church. Yet, he was concerned with civil authority when it was needed to either repel those who threatened him from reaching his desired reforms or when it was wrong in ruling the people.

The first concern of Luther was with the church and what she was doing to the faith. His insights into the real meaning of the gospel came to him while he was in the monastery. These insights helped him later in clarifying the issues which he was later to confront. At the beginning of his teaching career, he did not think of a reformation other than one in the classroom. But subsequent events came so fast that he was thrust into the role of the reformer. He was the pastor of a church and the members were buying indulgences. This he could not stand because it was inconsistent with his belief that man is justified by faith. Since man is justified by faith alone, why would he need to purchase indulgences to secure his salvation?

Though the church had practiced indulgences for years, Luther saw new dimensions added to their worth. The church had begun to beg as it never had before on the false notion that if one purchased indulgences he could gain rewards from the pope and even release someone from purgatory. This soliciting of monies from people had the approval of both the pope and the civil authority. The people were led to believe that the money was needed to build St. Peter's Basilica while, in truth, half of it went to the Fuggers and the other half to the pope. This fleecing of the land with so many poor was an abomination to all of Christianity.

Luther had observed this practice but never with so much extravagant pretensions made on behalf of indulgences as were made by Albert or Mainz. A summary of what was offered to those who bought are the following: (1) the plenary

remission of all sins, even those in purgatory; (2) a choice of a confessor fully empowered to absolve even the gravest of sins, even at death; (3) an indulgence ticket, even for the dead, which enables them to participate in benefits of the church here on earth; (4) and the remission of all sins to those souls in purgatory.[2]

Though to some in Wittenburg the appeal was captured in attractive language and approved by the pope, to Luther it was against the scriptures and his better judgment. As soon as he received a copy of Albert's instructions to the indulgence preachers, he was infuriated. In this mood, he confessed: "As certainly as Christ had redeemed me, I, just as other people, did not realize what indulgences were like."[3]

Luther responded to this abusive appeal in the tradition of his times by offering the *Ninety-Five Theses* for debate. These Theses were an attack upon the practice of indulgences. Selected ones from the long list illumine his proposals for debate.

(5) The pope neither desires nor is able to remit any penalties except those imposed by his own authority or that of the canons.

(8) The penitential canons are imposed only on the living, and according to the canons themselves, nothing should be imposed on the dying.

(21) Thus those indulgence preachers are in error who say that a man is absolved from every penalty and saved by papal indulgences.

(27) They preach only human doctrines who say that as soon as the money clinks into the money chest, the soul flies out of purgatory.

(28) It is certain that when money clinks in the money chest, greed and avarice can be increased; but when the church intercedes, the result is in the hands of God alone.

(29) Who knows whether all souls in purgatory wish to be re-

deemed, since we have exceptions in St. Severinus and St. Paschal, as related in a legend.

(30) No one is sure of the integrity of his own contrition, much less of having received plenary remission.

(40) A christian who is truly contrite seeks and loves to pay penalties for his sins; the bounty of indulgences, however, relaxes penalties and causes men to hate them—at least it furnishes occasion for hating them.

(45) Christians are to be taught that he who sees a needy man and passes him by, yet gives his money for indulgences, does not buy papal indulgences but God's wrath.

(50) Christians are to be taught that if the pope knew the exactions of the indulgence preachers, he would rather that the basilica of St. Peter were burned to ashes than built up with the skin, flesh, and bones of his sheep.

(56) The treasures of the church, out of which the pope distributes indulgences, are not sufficiently discussed or known among the people of Christ.

(62) The true treasure of the church is the most holy gospel of the glory and grace of God.

(94) Christians should be exhorted to be diligent in following Christ, their head, through penalties, death, and hell.[4]

Had the church not responded as it did to Luther, the proposals in the Theses may have just been another intellectual debate. But the church insisted that he who does not accept the authority of the pope and the doctrine he expounds is a heretic.[5] Little did Luther know at this time that the structures of which he was a part would force him to look at them in light of his newly discovered faith. He seemed destined not only to speak out against them but to demand a change in them. Thus, he offers a program for reform in his treatise "The Babylonian Captivity of the Church." To view Luther as reformer, I shall use this work

as a basic guide, drawing upon other areas of his writings as they are helpful in enlarging his role.

Luther raises the question as to the right of the church to claim the authority to give grace. For him, however, only God can do that. The Roman church, with its structures of councils and bishops, was subject to error.

Let this then stand first: The church can give no grace; that is the work of God alone. Therefore she cannot institute a sacrament. But even if she could, it still would not necessarily follow that ordination is a sacrament. For who knows which church is the church that has the Spirit? For when such decisions are made there are usually only a few bishops and scholars present; and it is possible that these may not be really the church. All may err, as councils have repeatedly erred, particularly the Council of Constance, which erred most wicked of all.[6]

This is a warning from Luther to the church not to equate the rules of the pope and councils with the rule of scripture and the God who inspired it. Luther respected the church fathers, particularly Augustine; but he did not equate their opinions with the work of God. In his criticism of Peter Lombard, this is clearly seen, for, in his classroom lectures, he used them to document his positions; but they, too, were not beyond his analysis. In speaking of Lombard:

Therefore, read with great caution the "Master of the Sentences" in his fourth book; better yet, despise him with all his commentators, who at their best write only of the "matter" and "form" of the sacraments; that is, they treat of the dead and death-dealing letter (II Cor. 3:6) of the sacraments, but leave untouched the spirit, life, and use, that is, the truth of the divine promise of our faith.[7]

Faith is the central theme of Luther's argument here. He does not leave out works; he desires that the Christian need not worry about them. Men were not to be deceived by "the external pomp of works and the deceits of man-made ordinances . . . lest you wrong the divine truth and your faith."[8]

Luther saw in the pope's actions and those of the clergy

an effort to usurp the place of the church. Having been a monk, he understood all too well how important the clergy was to the maintenance of the ecclesiastical authority to which he had to give account for his actions. If that structure could be reformed, the pope would have difficulty in holding control alone over the church. This papist attitude pervaded throughout the ordained ministers who were over the laity. In 1522, Luther developed a theory which made the whole concept of the ministry rest on the belief of the priesthood of believers. This meant that each man was his brother's priest. For him, neither the pope nor the ones whom he ordained had any more authority than any Christian who was baptized. "Let everyone, therefore, who knows himself to be a Christian, be assured of this, that we are all equally priest, that is to say, we have the same power in respect to the word and the sacraments."[9] This right the pope had taken away and "he seeks only to oppress us with his tyrannical power."[10] The people should have the right to select and approve of a priest if it meant someone who was not ordained by the Catholic church.

In his doctrine "Concerning the Ministry," he elaborates this position: "The authority and the dignity of the priesthood resided in the community of the believers."[11] The authority for the priesthood lay not in the rigors of monastic life, nor in the power of tyrannical popes, but in the scriptures. The presbyter or minister was given authority externally, but the priest was born to the Spirit.[12] The ministries of the church belonged to all the Christians.

The other area of the priesthood which concerned Luther was the school known as the monastery. Whereas Luther was an Augustinian monk, he did not encourage anyone else to commit himself to that way of life. This school with all its vows was to be avoided if the person who entered was not aware beforehand that his works in the monastery were no more value in the sight of God than those of the common laborer.[13] "Vows were against the faith" in Luther's view.[14] The monastic way of life then was set up in such a way as to

provide the monks with a way of works to sainthood or salvation. This did not give the monk an opportunity to actualize his faith through a life in the world.

Gustaf Wingren has observed how the monastic life functioned during Luther's times:

Monastic piety required monks to construct tribulations resembling Christ's "passion, i.e., mortification." But these tribulations were imitative attempts in which the edification of the monk was the main point. His purely human relationship with his fellowman was not part of the mortification; the need of his neighbor in no way influenced the monk's self-discipline or vice versa. Luther combines these two points, serving one's neighbor and bearing one's cross, and places this combined act in the world.[15]

As we shall see later, the biblical meaning of vocation was to be equated with the sixteenth-century man's everyday life. But the councils and the pope had invented a way of life diametrically opposed to this understanding. The monastic life cut off man's liberty and the possibility of freedom according to the gospel. In essence, a life of poverty, obedience, and chastity may be observed by a person's own choosing. In Luther's belief, these practices should never be superficially lived or demanded.[16] Having been a faithful monk himself, he could speak with some degree of authority on the slavery within the monastery and the freedom without.

In his address "To the Christian Nobility of the German Nation Concerning the Reform of the Christian Estate," Luther calls upon the ruling class to reform the church. He does this because, in his estimation, the pope and his councils have failed to take the necessary steps to do so, particularly with regard to the monastic order and its devastating mendicant orders. The execution of these orders invented by the church had already made Italy barren; and now they were about to make Germany the same way. The poor were not being cared for while the cardinals and the pope's secretaries were rich with lands and luxury. Luther describes the conditions and the people's need to be vigilant:

Now that Italy is sucked dry, the Romanists are coming into Germany. They have made a gentle beginning. But let us keep our eyes open. Germany shall soon be like Italy. We have few cardinals already. The "drunken Germans" are not supposed to understand what the Romanists are up to until there is not a bishopric, a monastery, a living, a benefice, not a red cent left. Antichrist must seize the treasures of the earth, as it is prophesied (Dan. 11:39, 43). . . . They then tear off a little piece each year so as to make quite a tidy sum after all. The priory of Wurzburg yields a thousand gulden; the priory of Bambery also yields a sum; Mainz, Trier, and others. In this way one thousand or ten thousand gulden may be collected, so that a cardinal could live like a wealthy monarch at Rome.[17]

Germany and its people to this time had to stand for this fleecing of its land and people. They had to: there was little choice for the peasants. They were giving more than their share to Rome while "we get nothing for it except scorn and contempt."[18] Yet there were those who continued "wondering why princes and nobles, cities and endowments, land and people, grow poor."[19] It was then the duty of the ruling people of the secular order to reform for themselves what the pope and Rome had failed to do. Luther based his argument on the belief that those who ruled had just as much authority to reform since they were Christians also. And as Christians they were priests and should do so. "They should rule the people entrusted to them in temporal and spiritual matters and protect them from these rapacious wolves in sheep's clothing who pretend to be their shepherds and rulers."[20]

Matters of such serious concern should not be left to popes and councils to decide; but they should be decided in open councils called by the prince and the people. For, in most cases, when councils were called to determine major issues, the pope had already decided the results in advance. And some of these issues affected the economic status of the German people. These councils, for the most part, had only a few persons there to rubber-stamp the pope's wishes.[21] Therefore, the prince and the other temporal rulers should

resist this robbing of the land and set up councils which would be free to meet the needs of the most people. The councils with their medicants should be regulated to the needs of the people.

It is far more important to consider what the common people need for their salvation than what St. Francis, St. Dominic, and St. Augustine, or anyone else has established as a rule, especially because things have not turned out as they planned.[22]

It was necessary for the German nation to resist this system of robbery from the hand of the pope: "Such power is not to be obeyed, but rather resisted with life, property, and with all our might and main."[23]

As Luther had made baptism the basis for authentic priesthood rather than ordination, he found himself faced with the charge of the Anabaptists that faith was necessary prior to baptism.[24] In "The Babylonian Captivity of the Church," he had made provisions for this charge. Infant baptism was valid in that what God promises always remains perpetual. "For the truth of the promise once made remains steadfast, always ready to receive us back with open arms when we return."[25] The promise of God conferred in his word at baptism was sure, even if man later in his life forfeited his commitment to God. From God's side, baptism can be correct and sufficient. In his writing, "In Concerning Rebaptism," he says:

But verily baptism can be correct and sufficient even if the Christian falls from faith or sins a thousand times a year. It is enough that he rights himself and becomes faithful, without having to be rebaptized each time. Then why should not the first baptism be sufficient and proper if a person truly becomes a believing Christian?[26]

The Anabaptists were dealing with the abuse of the sacrament rather than with the promise of God, the latter being the essential thing for Luther. They were doing the same thing that the papacy had done before him—relying on

works.[27] To rebaptize over and over again was a guise of faith which led people to rely on works. Baptism was a gift, just as faith was through grace. It was not to be made into a work. And this gift opened the baptized to the possibility of faith.

Luther's proposals for reform are always in opposition to those who would use the faith to lead people to rely on works. This was true in response to the Anabaptists. It is also true in his response to the way the church uses the Word of God and the sacraments. And it is an important observation in Luther's reforms that his experiences are in opposition to the papist errors concerning the scriptures. In "The Babylonian Captivity of the Church," he accuses the pope of tyranny in perverting the Word of God. The pope and his colleagues put their own interpretation on the gospel, making man-made laws which he expects the people to obey.

This impious and desperate tyranny is fostered by the pope's disciples, who here twist and pervert that saying of Christ. "He who hears you hears me" (Luke 10:16). With puffed cheeks they inflate this saying to a great size in support of their own ordinances.[28]

As long as the pope taught the gospel of Christ, he was to be followed and believed. But when he used his authority and his own words, he was not to be heeded. "Therefore, no one is obliged to obey the ordinances of the pope, or required to listen to him, except when he teaches the gospel and Christ."[29] The gospel was to be taught in freedom and without the restrictive and dogmatic elements of the papacy, for there was a distinct difference between the Word of God and the word of man.

We must make a great difference between God's Word and the word of man. A man's word is a little sound, that flies into the air, and soon vanishes; but the Word of God is greather than heaven and earth, yea, greater than death and hell, for it forms part of the power of God, and endures everlasting; we should, therefore, diligently study God's Word, and know and assuredly believe that God himself speaks to us.[30]

What then is the gospel of Christ for Luther, and how is it to be used? Luther answers this question in "The Freedom of a Christian":

> I answer: The apostle explains this in Romans 1. The Word is the gospel of God concerning his Son, who was made flesh, suffered, rose from the dead, and was glorified through the Spirit who sanctifies. To preach Christ means to feed the soul, make it righteous, set it free, and save it, provided it believes the preaching. Faith alone is the saving and efficacious as the Word of God, according to Rom. 10 [:9].[31]

Those scriptures that did not give precedence to faith over works are not apostolic. This distinction is made in Luther's analysis between James and Paul. He, therefore, wrote in the introductory paragraph of his Preface: "I think highly of the epistle of James, and regard it as valuable although it was rejected in early days. It does not expound human doctrine, but lays much emphasis on God's law."[32] Though he accepted James's epistle, he felt it showed a weakness in overemphasizing works in the scheme of faith. Works came as the result of faith.

Luther's attack on the sacraments of the church would agree with Adolf Harnack that Luther "cut the roots of the whole catholic notion of the sacraments."[33] As we have observed, Luther elevated the Word of God over every sacrament. It was upon this basis that all sacraments would either stand or fall. Again, in "The Babylonian Captivity of the Church," there are basically two sacraments that stand the analysis of the scriptures. These were baptism and the Lord's Supper. Luther, however, did not rule out prayer, work, and absolution. These were necessary, though he could not find scriptural proof for confessions.

Baptism, however, which we have applied to the whole of life, will truly be sufficient for all the sacraments which we might need as long as we live. And the bread is truly the sacrament of the dying and the departing; for if we commemorate the passing of Christ out of this world, that we may imitate him. Thus we may apportion

these two sacraments as followers; baptism may be allocated to the beginning and the entire course of life, while bread belongs to the end and to death. And the Christian should use them both as long as he is in this mortal frame. . . .[34]

In affirming his stance on the two sacraments, he did not rule out confession as a valuable tool for the Christian. He would not abolish it: "Indeed, I rejoice that it exists in the church of Christ, for it is a cure without equal for distress consciences."[35] It would be safe to conclude that Luther held to the value of confessions because of his own experiences of inward struggle and his need to express that struggle in relation to another human being. This is supported by his relationship with Johann von Staupitz. Roland H. Bainton says, "No one better could have been found as a spiritual guide. The vicar knew all the cures prescribed by the schoolmen for spiritual ailments, and besides had a warm religious life of his own with a sympathetic appreciation of the distress of another."[36] This also finds support in his doctrine on the priesthood of all believers. Each man should be a priest to his brother. In this kind of relationship, one could possibly hear the words of God through a brother. For Luther, such comfort could not be replaced by abolishing the confessions.

A careful examination of all of Luther's proposals for reform will indicate that he was a reformer. He did not attempt to overthrow the Catholic church by violence or force. He looked at the abuses of the church in light of the scriptures. This was also true, as we shall see later, in his dealings with the state.

The revolutionary, on the other hand, seeks to bring about change by whatever means may be necessary. He seeks to overthrow the existing order, either to replace it with an improved one or, in some cases, a more evil system. In most instances, he opposes constituted authority. Crane Brinton describes the revolutionist in clear examples:

Let us take a random list of names as they come to mind.

Hampden, Sir Henry Vane, John Milton, Sam Adams, John Hancock, Washington, Thomas Paine, Lafayette, Danton, Robespierrre, Marat, Talleyrand, Hervert, Miluikau, Konovalov, Kerensky, Chicherin, Lenin and Stalin. All are revolutionists; all opposed constituted authority with force of arms.[37]

Those who are revolutionaries do not appear from out of nowhere. There must be conditions which give rise to such figures. Luther's times were no different from any other times which produced revolutionaries. The conditions which thrust a Martin Luther into the role of reformer also motivated the peasants and Thomas Muntzer to respond as they did. The fleecing of the land by the church and the state, the subservient level to which the poor had been consigned to live, their lack of participation in the political structures, the lack of justice accorded to them in the courts, and a lack of community control—all were contributing factors in the peasant's rebellion. Friedrich Engels observes the unbearable conditions of the peasants, the very ingredients for revolt:

At the bottom of all the classes, save the last one, was the huge exploited masses of the nation, the peasants. It was the peasant who carried the burden of all the other strata of society; princes, officialdom, nobility, clergy, patricians and middle class. Whether the peasant was the subject of a prince, an imperial baron, a bishop, a monastery or a city, he was everywhere treated as a beast of burden, and worse. If he was a serf, he was entirely at the mercy of his master. If he was a bondsman, the legal deliveries stipulated agreement were sufficient to crush him: even they were being daily increased. Most of the time, he had to work on his master's estate. Out of that which he earned in his few free hours, he had to pay tithes, dues, ground rent, war taxes, land taxes, imperial taxes and other payments. He could neither marry nor die without paying the master. . . .[38]

These conditions extended to the control of property, and even over the peasant's person. Marriage among peasants was abused and disrespected by the masters. Every area of the peasant's life was controlled from above by some baron,

priest, or some patrician who knew full well what they were getting paid for.[39] They were being paid to exploit, control, and keep the peasant quiet. There was no one to defend and plead the cause of the peasants. Luther was pleading the cause of the German church. Some of his proposals for reform, both to the German ruling class and to the Roman church, would have benefited the peasants, but only as a by-product of his desired goals. Yet, they felt in Luther's attack on the structures of the church and its exploitation of the poor and the German nation, a degree of support for what they themselves were fighting for. Kyle C. Sessions supports this contention:

In 1524–25, Luther's gospel message was interpreted by them to serve as a bridge joining these two revolutionary systems. When he renewed Christ's message of human equality, he went against the medieval order in which inequality had been sanctioned as the penality for sin. Then Luther attacked the church, making its wealth and power suspect. Thereupon the struggle for the ancient law was joined easily to the struggle for the divine law to form a vision in the peasant minds. They foresaw the restoration of their faith and their life along ancient, proven lines.[40]

The peasants obviously believed that if there was an overthrow of papal authority there could be a return to an order of life which could not deprive them of their God-given and natural rights. There were, alongside these thoughts, the conservatives of that day who longed for the good old days which never were.[41] Yet the peasants were fed up with abstractions; they wanted concrete measures because their needs were concrete. From their "Twelve Articles," we can see a real concern for those necessities which had so long been denied them. This was mixed, however, with the desire for Divine rule. Excerpts from the "Twelve Articles" give us some indications of what they desired.

Articles one, two, eleven, and twelve basically dealt with religious matters based on scripture and divine order. Here they wanted the right to elect their own pastor and regulate

their giving. The peasants were willing to give to the church so long as it was consistent with scriptures. But when it came to man's inventions, they would no longer cooperate.

The First Article. First, it is our humble petition and desire, as also our will and resolution, that in the future we should have power and authority so that each community should choose and appoint a pastor, and that we should have the right to depose him should he conduct himself improperly. . . .

The Second Article. According as the just tithe is established by the Old Testament and fulfilled in the new, we are ready and willing to pay the tithe of grain.[42]

These articles are reminiscent of Luther's own argument for reform. Articles three, four, five, seven, eight, and ten dealt with the natural rights of man. It is clear here that the peasants wanted the liberty to hunt and fish, forest rights, equality, and release from overtaxation. They were tired of being overworked, overtaxed, and treated as though they were slaves. They were asking for community control based on the scriptures. The peasants wanted to respond to life as they interpreted it revealed in the Bible as is set forth in articles eleven and twelve.

The peasants, then, were concerned with economic and social issues as well as spiritual ones. Those things which affected their lives here and now were of uttermost importance.

The Third Article. . . . We therefore, take it for granted that you will release us from serfdom as true Christians, unless it should be shown as from the Gospel that we are serfs.

The Fourth Article. In the fourth place it has been the custom therefore, that no poor man should be allowed to catch venison or wild fowl or fish in flowing water, which seems to us quite unseemly and unbrotherly as well as selfish and not agreeable to the Word of God. . . .

The Fifth Article. In the fifth place we are aggrieved in the matter of wood-cutting, for the noble folk have appropriated all the woods to themselves alone. . . .

The Sixth Article. Our sixth complaint is in regard to the excessive services demanded of us which are increased from day to day.[43]

Article nine is of great importance when we observe how serfdom and slavery are maintained in all cultures. Whenever a people have been subjected, it takes legal as well as religious restrictions to continue such a system; those who are in power only bend to the will of the people when it is advantageous to their own special interest. Usually, when the slave learns the law and is able to use it effectively against the oppressor, the oppressor changes the law to suit his own purpose, or makes a new one to further frustrate the slave.

The Ninth Article. In the ninth place we are burdened with a great evil in the constant making of new laws. We are not judged according to the offence, but sometimes with great ill will, and sometimes much too leniently. In our opinion we should be judged according to the old written law so that the case shall be decided according to its merits, and not with partiality.[44]

It is clear what the rulers are doing. They show mercy only when it is in their own best interest. The law has a double standard when it is applied. It is no wonder the "Peasant's War Cry" was heard over and over again for almost a century before the Reformation. Though in sporadic manifestations of insurrections, they were nonetheless heard. And we must agree with Gunther Franz, that "one after another, savage and desperate insurrections broke out from Alsace, to the Tiral, and from the Black Forest into Franconia, Hess and Thuringia."[45] At the time of Luther's Reformation, the peasants intensified their sporadic revolts. Men began to lose respect for earning a living by the sweat of their brows because they found no meaning for life in working under such conditions as those of the peasants. They were reminiscent of the black slaves on the plantation. Labor no longer had meaning and dignity. "For the most part, rebels roamed the countryside in armed mobs, living off the

land, attracted by violence and loot—the modern race riots in America have some similarities and affinities as explosions of violence."[46] Some of the peasants began to view life as some blacks are doing today. For when they lost the meaningfulness of work and their dignity because of the treatment, they resorted to tricking the white man. They did as little as possible to survive. As Eldridge Cleaver put it in our time:

I think anyone who can beat that system and draw a living from it with the least expenditure of energy is doing the best thing he can do for himself. It is stupid to be a dedicated, hard-working and loyal victim. But if black people were in a situation where their labor had meaning and dignity, where they were really building good lives for themselves and their children, then all this strategic behavior would cease to be functional.[47]

The peasants had lost their sense of dignity in work for work's sake alone. They began to revolt. Sometimes it was against civil authority; at other times it was against the abusive authority of the churches upon the lands and people. Yet, underneath it all was the common age-old burden of outright oppression. Where the upper classes could fend for themselves, the poor people were left to suffering because of the restrictive measures which we have seen cited in the "Twelve Articles." Joseph Lortz considers these articles "as the most single demonstration of the connection between peasant upheaval and the sixteenth century Reformation."[48] The connection here is that if the reformers were advocating an equal share for all in the whole realm of Christian existence, then how did they view the poor oppressed peasants? As Lortz says:

Now if the struggle for freedom from subordination was overall at hand, so was there nonetheless no class so oppressed as the peasants and so without some manner of sufficient share in common rights. What everyone was taking up, therefore, could very well work convincingly on them.[49]

Though the peasants may have found in the reformers a sense of freedom from subordination, they certainly differed from their methodology on reaching their desired goals. Their articles were biblical enough, and what they were asking for was what they should have had all along. But what they did not seem to have was someone to give direction to their movement. Being unlettered as they were, they were easy prey for the left-wingers of the Reformation. Preacher after preacher came and went without giving any good strategic planning to the peasant's Revolt. As Gordon Rupp has said, "there were very few systematic programs and not many leaders."[50] Yet there was one Thomas Muntzer, who "was interested in economic amelioration only for the sake of religion, and he did have the insight to see what no one else in his generation observed, that faith itself does not thrive on physical exhaustion."[51]

Muntzer more than any other preacher sought to give some sense of direction to the peasant movement. He attempted to develop a theology for revolution. He actually gave the peasants a reason to choose violence as a means for achieving their desired goals. With this interpretation of the scripture, he justified for the peasants the use of violence. It is understandable why the peasants needed a Thomas Muntzer when we observe what Luther was teaching. And it was out of Muntzer's reaction to Luther's passive approach to political and social concerns that Muntzer developed a more thoroughgoing theology of violence. This is seen in his clear perception of the horrible conditions under which the peasants lived and Luther's attitude toward temporal authority.

Luther says that the poor people have enough in their faith. Doesn't he see that usury and taxes impede the reception of the faith? He claims that the word of God is sufficient. Doesn't he realize that men whose every movement is consumed in the making of a living have no time to learn to read the Word of God? The princes bleed the people with usury and count as their own the fish in the stream, the bird in the air, and the grass of the field, and Dr. Lair says, "Amen!" What courage has he, Dr. Pussyfoot, the new Pope of

Wittenberg, Dr. Easychair, the basking sycophant? He says there should be no rebellion because the sword has been committed by God to the ruler, but the power of the sword belongs to the whole community. In the good old days the people stood by when judgment was rendered lest the ruler pervert justice, and the rulers have perverted justice. They shall be cast down from their seats. The fowls of the heavens are gathering to devour their carcasses.[52]

Ralph Z. Moellering holds that Muntzer's choice to use violence as a means to achieve his goals was the result of his contact with the mystic Nicholas Storch. Moellering believes that:

He adapted and expanded Storch's expectation that the people chosen by God, the true Christians, would rise up and exterminate all the godless. These ruthless and destructive actions were necessary prelimaries to the second advent of Christ and the inauguration of the millennium.[53]

This analysis is in agreement with Crane Brinton's anatomy of the revolutionist when we consider Muntzer's approach to revelation. Muntzer believed that revelation was still in progress and that God revealed himself to the chosen. He denounced education, though he was an educated man himself. He admired Luther as his spiritual father in the ministry. Yet, he left Luther soon after he met him. Crane Brinton would call these actions revolutionary traits of the "misguided superiors":

They see the possibilities of a better world. They are influenced by the writings of the intellectuals, who have begun their desertion of the established order. They begin to feel acutely their differences from their fathers and grandfathers; they are a generation in revolt. They come to struggle for God's Kingdom on earth.[54]

This is exactly what Muntzer expected and what he preached. With his eschatological strategy, he went before the peasants in war holding the peasants' banners high. These banners consisted of "a white flag with a sword and a

great white banner with a rainbow symbolic of the new convenant."[55] He had come indeed to believe that the peasant uprisings were the end of the fifth monarchy prophesied in Daniel and later by himself in the great sermon before the princes. With his faith, Muntzer turned all of his attention to the concerns of the peasants and interpreting the scriptures in view of the revolution that was going on.

Luther believed that the kingdom was near, but he was not so bent on bringing about the second advent of Christ by force as Muntzer was. This is evident in his reaction "Against the Murdering and Thieving Hordes of Peasants":

For if a man is in open rebellion, everyone is both his judge and his executioner; just as when a fire starts, the first man who can put it out is the best man to do the job. For rebellion is not just simple murder; it is like a great fire, which attacks and devastates a whole land. Thus rebellion brings with it a land filled with murder and bloodshed; it makes widows and orphans, and turns everything upside down, like the worst disaster. Therefore let everyone who can, smite, slay, and stab, secretly or openly, remembering that nothing can be more poisonous, hurtful, or devilish than a rebel. It is just as when one must kill a mad dog; if you do not strike him, he will strike you, and a whole land with you.[56]

As we listen to Luther's call to control and kill the peasants, one wonders what has happened to the Luther who advocated that the only weapon he would use was the Word of God. Did he forget so soon that it is those same princes and those same churchmen whom he denounced as responsible for the problems of the poor people? Did he expect human beings whose souls had been crushed for so long would forever endure such harsh oppression without some form of redress? Obviously, Luther was caught in the middle of a struggle and did not know how to respond. He did not know where he should stand. In one breath he told the princes to kill the peasants, and in the other breath he chastised the princes for being so ruthless. At best, Luther is a religious leader and is out of place in dealing with a social revolution.

Without tracing the further detailed movement of Thomas Muntzer, it should be sufficient to state his primary position on the interpretation of the scriptures on the use of violence, and observe where those ideas led him and the Peasant Rebellion. Muntzer set forth most eloquently his position in the "Sermon Before the Princes" of Allstedt in 1534.

For the godless person has no right to live when he is in the way of the pious. In Ex. 22:18 God says: Thou shalt not suffer evildoers to live. Saint Paul also means this where he says the sword of the rulers that is bestowed upon them for the retribrution of the wicked as protection for the pious (Rom. 13:4)[57]

This interpretation more than any other was used to justify violence as a means to an end. Muntzer led the peasants in their last revolt at Frankenhausen, where they were all slaughtered by the thousands. Suffice it to say, the only ones who profited from the Peasants' Revolt were the princes. Their rule was strengthened and the peasants were given little if any participation in political life. This cause was set back for a long time to come. Muntzer was caught and later executed for his role in the rebellion. The peasants' guns were taken away and the princes took the freedom to control them more forcefully. These events remind us of our situation in the United States today. The riots following the Civil Rights movement of the last decade were used by the government and the police departments as a justification for passing new gun control laws and for a massive rearming of the local law enforcement agencies.

Whatever Muntzer did, at least he, more than any other reformer, raised the question of how far a Christian should go in dealing with an oppressive government. More than any other man of his day, he laid bare the smothered undercurrents of the medieval pains of injustice. His voice was hushed for a long time until it was again heard in these latter days in Dietrich Bonhoeffer's role in the assassination

plot to kill Adolf Hitler. He further gave the theologians the chance to wrestle with the question of to what extent civil disobedience can play a role in liberating an oppressed people.

The use of civil disobedience as a way of liberation of an oppressed people was used in this country most effectively by Martin Luther King, Jr. Martin Luther King attempted to use civil disobedience to break down the barriers of segregation and integrate the American black man into the main stream of this society. To reform this society, King felt that segregation had to be removed once and for all. Segregation was an evil that had to be rooted out. He had no illusion, however, on the way this had to be done. Martin Luther King believed that if we were to overcome the brokenness of our nation, the estrangement of brother from brother, we had to do it within the framework of the present system of government. Though America had perverted the ideas of this democracy, he always had hope that, with God and man's capacities working together, evil could be eradicated. Of this hope he writes:

Ever since the signing of the Declaration of Independence, America has manifested a schizophrenic personality on a question of race. She has been torn between selves—a self in which she has proudly professed democracy and a self in which she has sadly practiced the antithesis of democracy. The reality of segregation, like slavery, has always had to confront the ideals of democracy and Christianity.[58]

He felt that we could change the present trend of this nation by using Gandhi's method of nonviolent resistance to evil with the ethic of Jesus known as love. If anything could remedy the situation, that process could. And it was these influences that ultimately brought Martin Luther King to his work as reformer rather than that of a revolutionary.

The first of these influences, however, came when King was very young. He recalls that he grew up with a bitter dislike for segregation and those who oppressed black people and poor whites. "I had passed spots where Negroes had been

savagely lynched and had watched the Ku Klux Klan on its rides at nights. I had seen police brutality with my own eyes and watched Negroes receive the most tragic injustice in the courts."[59] These conditions inspired him to engage in an intellectual search to help find solutions to the problems of segregation and racism in the society. Unlike Martin Luther, the German reformer, King did not suffer directly from economic deprivation; his family was relatively well-off. His father was a Baptist minister with a large congregation. Yet, Martin Luther King, Jr., could not look upon the economic exploitation of his people, or any people, for that matter, without feeling that he was somehow involved in that suffering. While working in a plant, he saw firsthand the injustices which were laid upon the blacks and whites alike. "Here I saw economic injustice firsthand, and realized that the poor white was exploited just as the Negro."[60] These experiences perhaps broadened his perspective as far as his concern for all people. He stated himself that at one time in his life, "I had come perilously close to resenting all white people."[61]

However, until he was sure of where he could best help his downtrodden people, he would not commit himself to any particular field of endeavor.[62] In his college career, he read Thoreau's "Essay on Civil Disobedience" and was gripped by what Thoreau had to say about refusing to cooperate with evil. "I was so deeply moved that I reread the work several times. This was my first intellectual contact with the theory of nonviolent resistance."[63] After college, King began to study the great ethical and social philosophers—Plato, Aristotle, Rousseau, Hobbes, Bentham, Mill, and Locke. All of these stimulated King's thinking, but they did not satisfy his quest for a method to solve the problems of his people. The quest continued through Karl Marx, where he learned something about the evils of captialism based on the profit and gain motive. In such a system, those who were in power could take advantage of the weak and the poor. King rejected Marx, however, because he made the state an end in

itself: "Man becomes hardly more in communism, than a de-personalized cog in the turning wheel of the state."[64] And later Marxist interpreters saw in Marx's philosophy the right to use any means necessary to reach the goal of a classless society. For Martin Luther King, the individual was important and he was never to be sacrificed for the state. The state was here to serve man rather than man to serve the state.[65]

He learned a great deal from the ethical and social philosophers, but it was not until he met the teachings of Walter Rauschenbush's *Christianity and the Social Crisis* that he found a theological basis for his social concern. Though he could not accept the temptation in Rauschenbush to equate the Kingdom of God with a kind of social and economic interaction, he nevertheless felt that Rauschenbush had made a significant contribution.

But in spite of these shortcomings, Rauschenbush gave to American Protestantism a sense of social responsibility that it should never lose. The gospel at its best deals with the whole man, not only his soul but also his body, not only his spiritual well-being but also his material well-being.[66]

This position gave King a theological basis for his early, ever-present social concern for the person. Any religion, then, "that professes a concern for the souls of men and is not equally concerned about the slums that damn them, the economic conditions that cripple them, is a spiritually moribund religion."[67] Religion for King was of little value if it did not concern itself with the conditions and evils that destroy the soul of man and treat the poor unjustly. The Christian faith was born in protest against such injustices.[68] Yet, King had some misgivings about the power of love to eradicate evil. He almost despaired at this: "During this period I had almost despaired of the power of love to solve the social problems."[69] Thus, he had to find a more realistic way to apply this power of which the gospel spoke.

In Philadelphia, King heard Dr. Mordecai Johnson deliver an address on the life and teaching of Mahatma Gandhi. Of Dr. Johnson's message King wrote later, "His message was so profound and electrifying that I left the meeting and bought a half-dozen books on Gandhi's life and works."[70] As he studied Gandhi's method of nonviolent resistance, his difficulty in believing in the power of love began to decrease.

As I read I became deeply fascinated by his campaigns of nonviolent resistance. I was particularly moved by the Salt March to the Sea and his numerous fasts. The whole concept of "Satyagrapha" [means truth-force or love-force] therefore, was profoundly significant to me. As I delved deeper into the philosophy of Gandhi my skepticism concerning the power of love gradually diminished, and I came to see for the first time its potency in the area of social reform.[71]

With this understanding, Martin Luther King found a method by which he could apply the love ethic found in the teachings of Jesus to bring about reform. King knew that black people could not win the necessary reforms by violent means because they were ill-equipped and ill-trained to confront a militarily armed society. Gandhi's technique was the only effective way for an oppressed people. As Gandhi himself put it:

In the application of Satyagrapha I discovered in the earliest stages that pursuit of truth did not admit of-violence being inflicted on one's opponent but that he must be weaned from error by patience and sympathy. For what appears to be truth to the one may appear to be error to the other. And patience means self-suffering. So the doctrine came to mean vindication of truth not by infliction of suffering on the opponent but on one's self.[72]

As Martin Luther was helped by St. Augustine's understanding of the way of faith, Martin Luther King was aided in his use of love by Gandhi's understanding of nonviolent resistance to evil. From Gandhi's use of nonviolent resis-

tance, King studied Niebuhr's critique of pacifism. But this still left King in a state of indecision and confusion.[73] Passive resistance in Niebuhr seemed to suggest that there was no difference between violent and nonviolent resistance if the group against whom the resistance was directed had no moral conscience.

Non-violent conflict and coercion may also result in destruction of life or property and they usually do. The difference is that destruction is not the intended but the inevitable consequence of nonviolent coercion. The chief difference between violence and nonviolence is not in the degree of destruction which they cause, though the difference is usually considerable, but in the aggressive character of the one and the negative character of the other.[74]

King, however, was able to discern the fallacy in Niebuhr's thought. For him it was not a question of the lesser of two evils, violence or nonviolence; rather it was true pacifism which was nonviolent resistance to evil.[75] It was as he saw in Thoreau's noncooperation with evil. To cooperate with evil was to be a part of the evil. And King would never do this. "To accept passively an unjust system is to cooperate with that system; thereby the oppressed become as evil as the oppressor."[76] Men were to struggle against evil systems in order to bring about change. And to do this effectively, Martin Luther King chose the way of nonviolent resistance with love at its center. As L.D. Reddick observed: "Three of King's heroes—Jesus, Thoreau and Gandhi—supply the philosophical roots for his own theory of non-violent social change."[77]

Armed with Gandhi's method and Jesus' spirit, Martin Luther King set out to attempt to make this nation actualize its ideals as they are written in the Declaration of Independence, the Bill of Rights, and the Constitution of the United States. This was also true when it came to reforms for the church, as we shall see later.

As Luther's understanding of faith came in direct conflict with the Roman church's perversion of that faith

through works' righteousness, Martin Luther King's understanding of justice came in direct conflict with this nation's perversion of justice through the propagation of unjust laws. For King there was nothing wrong with the ideals written in the Constitution, the Bill of Rights, or the Declaration of Independence; the problem was that now those who were in power misrepresented the intent of the ideals. And the greatest misuse of the law was segregation. King believed that this racist policy has corrupted the nation's democracy. "This long standing racist ideology had corrupted and diminished our democratic ideals."[78] And if this nation were to be true to its democratic ideals, then she would have to seek to reform herself and grant to all of her citizens equality under the law. There should not be a double standard of justice. There had to be equality for all.

With this position, Martin Luther King stood within the existing structures of American democracy and began to offer some suggestions for reform. King's reforms were directed toward making the written law of the land become a life experience for black people as it was for the white people. As has been stated, segregation was the foremost obstacle to this reality. Before the Negro could have equality, the monstrous policies of segregation and discrimination had to be removed.

First and foremost of his reforms was desegregation of the present facilities which already existed on an equal basis. This would offer the Negro an opportunity to have the same social mobility that whites have. In other words, King wanted for the Negro the same opportunities that white Americans had under the true ideas of democracy, for those man-made laws that were not in harmony with what he called the law of God or the moral law and the natural law were no laws at all. In an effort to illumine what he meant, he explained:

An unjust law is a code that a numerical or powerful majority group compels a minority group to obey but does not make it bind-

ing on itself. This is difference made legal. By the same token, a just law is a code that a majority is to follow and that is willing to follow itself. This is sameness made legal.[79]

And when this perversion of the law is allowed, the best method to insure the application of law equally for an oppressed people is through nonviolent civil disobedience. One should break the law out of his commitment to the higher law or moral law of God. But when he breaks the unjust law, he is willing to take the suffering and penalty it incurs. This process, King believed, would have the potential of transforming the oppressors. It would further purify the resister and draw public sympathy to the cause. As King contends:

We must seek democracy and not the substitution of one tyranny for another. Our aim must never be to defeat or humiliate the white man. We must not become victimized with a philosophy of black supremacy. God is not interested merely in the freedom of black men, and brown men, and yellow men; God is interested in the freedom of the whole human race.[80]

It was segregation and man-made laws which were in opposition to the intent of the Constitution that caused other manifestations of exploitation and discriminatory practices in the various areas of the black man's life. Particularly, this is true in the areas of education, economics, and housing.

Martin Luther King insisted on reforms in the educational structures of our society. The school, for him, "by and large, did not know how to teach—nor frequently what to teach."[81] He believed that the burden for financing adequate schools and facilities which would include the Negro should be borne by the federal government. King further held to the position that the Negro was excluded from the best education this country had to offer. Also, he believed that the separate-but-equal dogma could never solve the problem of a lack of quality education for the Negro. Therefore, the schools in the ghetto should be upgraded, but not at the expense of desegregation. To do this, we could use the existing

structures and temporary structures, a sort of educational park idea.[82]   With this concept, King desired that America should begin a creative approach to education which would stop wasting the human resource of the excluded Negro. Those who were poor—whether they were black or white, Mexican-American, or Indian—should be provided with such skills as were necessary to become productive, functional human beings. The unequal position which had existed between the Negro and the white had to be balanced by some special means of compensatory deeds for the harmed. The whole attitude of the nation had to be changed with respect to this idea. Speaking of the condition of blacks: "Often they are so far behind that they need more and special attention, the best quality education that can be offered."[83]

In addition to quality education for the poor, economics had its role to play. More and better jobs had to be found. Equality of opportunity in jobs should be given to the Negro. Training for these jobs should be conducted with a realistic approach. The gap between the haves and the have-nots had to be closed as soon as possible. Martin Luther King recognized the difficulty in proposing such. He knew that the critics would question his aggressiveness. When they agreed that equality was enough for the Negro, King had this to say:

Whenever this issue of compensatory or preferential treatment for the Negro is raised, some of our friends recoil in horror. The Negro should be granted equality, they agree; but he should ask nothing more. On the surface, this appears reasonable, but it is not realistic. For it is obvious that if a man is entered at the starting line in a race three hundred years after another man, the first would have to perform some impossible feat in order to catch up with his fellow runner.[84]

Thus, the one who had been harmed the most needed the most attention, for he who had been wounded worst by the national practices was the one to whom the nation was indebt-

ed the most. Without a realization of this attitude, the Negro would never catch up. Accordingly, King offered his Bill of Rights for the Disadvantaged. He believed that if Congress would pass such a bill, its psychological and motivational benefits to the Negro would be a transformation for him.[85] The poor whites would also benefit from such a creative approach. And it would help deliver the nation from the contradiction of poverty in the midst of so much plenty.

King was not naive about the law as was written and the law as it was practiced. If such a bill were to become actualized in the life of the poor, it would need vigorous enforcement by the federal government. He felt that the states and municipalities had in many instances nullified the Constitution. It was as in the time of medieval practices. To this point he concludes:

We find ourselves in a society where the supreme law of the land, the Constitution, is rendered inoperative in vast areas of the nation. State, municipal, and county laws and practices negate constitutional mandates as blatantly as if each community were an independent medieval duchy.[86]

Any program dealing with assistance for the poor would bring about strong resistance from the South and those special groups of the North. King knew that those programs would, therefore, need strong leadership from the executive branch, meaning the counsel of the president. In addition to this, the federal government would have to support the actualization of such programs with deliberate vigor. Resistance primarily based on fear and racism had always characterized the white man's position as his rationale for not granting the Negro his equal rights. White society had its emphasis on the wrong basis. The fear of intermarriage was unwarranted as a basis for not allowing integration. This was an individual concern between two people who consented to marriage. It had nothing to do with the collective evils of racism. These fears had to be done away with. So at this

point, King believed that we desperately needed an alliance with the federal government.[87]

On the economic front, jobs would have to be a top priority. King insisted that America had ignored the deep depression in the Negro community. With its paternalism and welfare assistance, it had dehumanized people.[88] We needed jobs, but in our effort to provide jobs there had previously been training prior to the actual employment. King wanted to reverse this trend because in many instances men were being trained for jobs that did not exist.[89] This procedure inevitably bred more frustration. It was the soil for revolt. It had a tendency to raise false hopes. To remedy this, there should be jobs first and training on the job. The government should subsidize those businesses which would employ the poor and unskilled. This implies that one would be paid while he was in training, thereby increasing his sense of dignity and respect for work.[90]

In his programs for reforms, Martin Luther King saw a need for the protection of the democratic rights which had already been won. Though we had won the right to vote, that right had to be protected. And we should move toward a deeper participation in the really major decision-making process of this nation, especially when it had to do with decisions that affected the lives of poor people.[91]

On housing, his position was essentially the same as it was with the schools and education. Though he advocated improvement of the slums, nothing was to be done at the expense of desegregation, for true desegregation was the key to making sure that the Negro got a fair share of the national life.

If these goals were pursued with vigor and sincerity by all interested groups of good will, the nation would possibly be saved from a racial war. Its democratic ideas would come to fruition, and its soul would be saved: "To end poverty, to extirpate prejudice, to free a tormented conscience, to make a tomorrow of justice, fair play and creativity—all these are worthy of the American ideal."[92]

MARTIN LUTHER–MARTIN LUTHER KING, JR.
AND THE BLACK EXPERIENCE

Martin Luther King was primarily a reformer because he often spoke of the American Dream as set forth in the laws of the founding fathers. He desired that America would square with its ideals—that is all. Whatever else he did, he passionately wanted the Negro to have his fair due. In this sense, he relates more to Luther and his concern for the German people as they struggled against the Roman church. On the other hand, while Luther moved away from the Roman church, Martin Luther King and the Negro tended to move toward the goal of full participation in the national life. King and the Negro wanted to be a part of the mainstream of society in the land where they had been nurtured and where they had suffered so agonizingly. King was determined to change America from within. To do this, the Negro needed alliances, since he was in a minority. In his final published statement, he wrote:

America has not yet changed because so many think it need not yet change, but this is the illusion of the damned. America must change because 23,000,000 black citizens will no longer live supinely in a wretched past. They have left the valley of despair; they have found strength in struggle; and whether they live or die, they shall never crawl nor retreat again. Joined by white allies, they will shake the prison walls until they fall. America must change.[93]

King did not live to see his dream come true, but on the eve of his assassination he was determined to see it through to fulfillment. The Promised Land was in his sight, and it really did not matter whether he got there with his people or not as long as they got there. A careful examination of his proposals for the Poor People's Campaign do not indicate that he planned to attempt to overthrow the government by violence or force.

His sense of history and his understanding of evil as it manifested itself in the structures of society convinced him that the only viable way to bring about the beloved community was through nonviolent militant protest based on love.

Man's potential for good and evil was too real for anyone to take it for granted. So it is wise, prudent, and expedient to appeal to the potential of good in man rather than to the evil by violent force. Change through violent means would have to come through some other group, but not through Martin Luther King, Jr.

These other groups took on a more revolutionary character. The times and conditions had outgrown, as it were, the accommodative approach of Booker T. Washington, the talented tenth which Du Bois felt to be the hope, the long legal battles of the NAACP, the moderate approach of the Urban League, and the nonviolent resistance of Martin Luther King. Nonviolent, direct action had been successful in the South; but this method in the North had only compelled businesses to hire a few Negroes. Black people were beginning to feel that King's approach and those of other Negro leaders were limited, useful instruments in the quest for freedom. Mass unemployment, underemployment, and police brutality still persisted. The slums were rat-infested and the mood began to change. The masses were still excluded from the tokenism granted by the pressures of the Civil Rights Movement. As economist Vivian Henderson clearly articulated before the U.S. Riot Commission:

No one can deny that all Negroes have benefited from civil rights laws and desegregation in public life in one way or another. The fact is, however, that the masses of Negroes have not experienced tangible benefits in a significant way. This is so in education and housing. It is critically so in the area of jobs and economic security. Expectations of Negro masses for equal job opportunity programs have fallen far short of fulfillment.

Negroes have made gains. . . . There have been important gains. But . . . the masses of Negroes have been virtually untouched by those gains.[94]

And the old-line civil rights organizations did not keep pace with their sons and daughters who had now outgrown their slow and arduous approach to solving the problems of

the Negro. By the midpoint of the sixties, members of groups such as SNCC and CORE, which had previously worked alongside the efforts of King and the NAACP, began to reject the middle-class goals as a way to freedom. Suspicious about white liberals and organized labor, they began to talk about such alliances as only temporary devices in the scheme of liberation. More than that, they saw such alliances as myths.[95]

Stokeley Carmichael more than anyone else elaborated this position. He viewed coalitions with perception and analysis. He believed that the goals of the black man would always be perverted if he attempted to enter a coalition with whites who had a condescending manner. Before we could talk of coalition, our goals should be well-defined first, within a group so cohesive that it could not be absorbed by any force.[96] Carmichael was echoing the admonition of Machiavelli:

And here it should be noted, that a prince ought carefully to avoid making common cause with any one more powerful than himself, for the purpose of attacking another power, unless he should be compelled to do so by necessity. For if the former is victorious, then you are at his mercy; and princes should, if possible, avoid placing themselves in such a position.[97]

The sons of the civil rights movement were now saying that Blacks should put themselves as little as possible in positions where they would need coalitions.

Traditionally, for each new ethnic group the route to social and political integration into America's pluralistic society has been through the organization of their own institutions with which to represent their communal needs within the larger society.[98]

It was a time as though everything had changed and nothing had changed. It was a time of hope and a time of frustration. It was a time of the signing of civil rights bills at the White House when those already in the lawbooks were being

perverted. "It is August 1619: 245 years before Emancipation, 346 years before the long hot summer of 1965."[99] There was talk of a new Negro now who talked of the need for revolutionary changes in the structures of American society. Coupled with the rhetoric were the shouts for retaliatory measures and the moving away from alliances with whites. As the frustration grew, the Negro felt that he had been misled in believing that America would grant him his rights. In view of this, only black power could rip from the white power structures what the black man deserved. The press played the rhetoric up without attempting to understand its full implications.

Ideology and pronouncements continued to flow and blacks became more angry. Malcolm X, more than anyone else, best articulated this mood. He grew up with the scar in his soul that whites had murdured his father in cold blood. He was able to see through all the untruths and perversions of justice. Finally, his position was that racism was so deep in the culture of the nation that it could not change. With this conviction, Malcolm sought to instill in the black people a sense of race pride and self-respect. His philosophy later broadened to a kind of Pan-Africanism that Du Bois had talked about many years before Malcom was born. This doctrine espoused the hope that people of color around the world, especially in Africa and Asia, would unite against the exploitation and colonialism of the Western white man.

Malcolm felt that to sing "We Shall Overcome" was all right, as long as you had a gun in your pocket for self-defense. As Malcolm spoke, no one knew the possible influence he was having on the young black mind. While the middle class by and large ignored him as another radical, others saw the merit of his truth. "But most Negroes, some of whom were very, very conservative, believed—and believe—that Malcolm's indictment, as distinguished from his proposed solutions, was a true bill."[100] As his leader Elijah Muhammund, he advocated separation from the white man. This position changed, as has been stated, to one of

Pan-Africanism. Malcolm used the mass media, especially the television, to reach the masses. And he constantly challenged the Negro leaders as to whether they represented the masses. This made the civil rights leaders struggle for the allegiance of the masses. Martin Luther King, Jr., had been catapulted to prominence by his success in Montgomery, Alabama, and other southern cities. He was considered a leader of black people, and leader he was. His sincerity and warmth were felt by all. It was he more than anyone else who offered hope of a desegregated future. The press had helped to make him such a symbol. His appeal to absorb suffering rather than inflict it was now getting unpopular to those who had practiced it and to those who had watched police brutality and felt k–9 dogs sink their furious teeth into their flesh.

In the midst of King's efforts, blacks were still being killed in the prime of their lives and nothing was being done about it except in isolated cases. President Kennedy, Medgar Evers, and Malcolm had all been murdered; James Meredith had been shot. Stokeley Carmichael confronted Martin Luther King to side with black power as the new slogan for the civil rights movement; he asked King to agree that there should be no whites in the continuation of the Meredith March. King refused because he felt that it "would confuse our allies, isolate the Negro community and give many prejudiced whites, who might otherwise be ashamed of their anti-Negro feeling, a ready excuse for self-justification."[101]

The consciousness which Malcolm had posited into the minds of young blacks had already taken root. On the day that Malcolm was killed, a Black Panther-to-be gave this as his reaction:

When Malcom X was killed in 1965, I ran down the street. I went to my mother's house, and I got six loose red bricks from the garden. I got to the corner, and broke the motherfuckers in half. I wanted to have the most shots that I could have, this very same day Malcolm was killed.[102]

Bobby Seale was to feel the death of Malcolm and also what he was saying. He was to talk about it, but it was not until he met Huey P. Newton that he understood what Malcolm was saying about self-defense and what Frantz Fanon was saying about organizing the *Lumpenproletariat*. The time had come for an end to police brutality and to the way of nonviolence as a way to freedom. Malcolm had given them a rationale to pick up the gun and Fanon had given them the reason to use it. Hope no longer rested in the hands of the middle-class Negro exploiters or the whites. As Fanon says:

During the struggle for freedom, a marked alienation from these practices is observed. The native's back is to the wall, the knife is at his throat [or, more precisely, the electrode at his genitals]: he will have no more call for his fancies. After centuries of unreality, after having wallowed in the most outlandish phantoms, at long last the native, gun in hand, stands face to face with the only forces which contend for his life—the forces of colonialism. And the youth of a colonised country, growing up in an atmosphere of shot and fire, may well make a mock of, and does not hesitate to pour scorn upon the zombies of his ancestors, the horses with two heads, the dead who rise again, and the djinns who rush into your body while you yawn. The native discovers reality and transforms it into a pattern of his customs, into the practice of violence and into his plan for freedom.[103]

Huey P. Newton taught Bobby Seale that what was important in life was not just to relate to Malcolm's personality but to "relate more to what Malcolm X was saying to do."[104] The time to implement the rhetoric into a practical program of action was now.

Newton understood that in order to organize the *Lumpenproletariat*—meaning the pimps, the hustlers, the guys on the block, the unemployed, the underemployed, the robbers, the ex-convicts—one had to offer them a program that they could relate to. That is what Fanon meant when he said, "If you don't do it the system will organize them

against you."[105] Armed with this understanding of Malcolm X and Frantz Fanon, Newton, Seal, and others forged their way through gang fights, through jiving black college intellectuals, through black culturalists, through confrontation after confrontation with police brutality, to the organization known as the Black Panther Party.

I think that it is extremely important here to point up the fact that Newton, the founder of the Party, picked up the gun within the confines of the law written in the Constitution of the United States. The Second Amendment says that every man has the right to bear arms. His intentions were primarily for self-defense purposes. In essence, he and the brothers were calling the nation back to a just use of the gun rather than the unjust use to which the police had put it. And since the cop had misused the gun by mistreating black people, they were now going to show the white racist how it was really to be used. They wanted to protect the black community from police brutality and terrorism. To do this, however, they needed a program to which the people could relate and understand. This took shape in September, 1966, in Oakland, California. Huey dictated and Bobby Seale wrote it down. This is a summary of how it appeared in their newspapers each week.

1. We want freedom. We want power to determine the destiny of our Black Community. . . .

2. We want full employment for our people. . . .

3. We want an end to the robbery by the white man of our Black Community. . . .

4. We want decent housing, fit for shelter of human beings. . . .

5. We want education for our people that espouses the true nature of this decadent American society. We want education that teaches us our true history and our role in the present day society. . . .

6. We want all black men to be exempt from military service. We believe that Black people should not be forced to fight in the military service to defend a racist government that does not protect us. . . . We will protect ourselves from the force and violence of the racist police and the racist military, by whatever means necessary.

7. We want an immediate end to POLICE BRUTALITY AND MURDER of black people.

We believe we can end police brutality in our black community by organizing black self-defense groups that are dedicated to defending our community from racist police oppression and brutality. The Second Amendment to the Constitution of the United States gives a right to bear arms. We therefore believe that all black people should arm themselves for self-defense.

8. We want freedom for all black men held in federal, state, county and city prisons and jails.[106]

The last two deal with the right to fair trials, land, freedom, and the natural necessities that any other citizen is entitled to. Finally, if these needs are not met by the existing government, the people have a right to replace it, as the Constitution indicates, with one that will.

A close examination of what the Black Panther Party wanted was what they should have had in view of how the black man had been treated in this country. Their programs and proposals incorporate some if not all that Martin Luther King, Jr., had asked for before they appeared. Surely, the whites were the first to dodge the draft and raid selective service offices to burn the records in their opposition to the war in Vietnam; but no police department or government agency had declared war on them because they were white.

As in the case of the peasants of Luther's time, it was not what they wanted that eventually brought about their destruction; it was the audacity of a black man to use the very means that whites had used to oppress him to win his freedom. It was the threat of the black man's arming himself for self-protection, let alone telling a white cop that "if you shoot at me I am going to shoot back at you."

In response to the Panther's manliness, the FBI and the police, the press, and television produced a national atmosphere that gave most of white America what they felt to be a justification for killing them. William Schulz gives this view of the nation's feeling toward the Panthers:

The Black Panther Party, a virulent, self-styled "armed revolutionary vanguard." In less than two years, the Panthers have mushroomed from a 125-man contingent based solely in Oakland, Calif., to a nationwide operation with 60,000 sympathizers and chapters in two dozen cities. "Schooled in Marxist-Leninist ideology and the teachings of Mao Tse-tung," reports the FBI, "Panther members have perpetrated and engaged in violent confrontations with police throughout the country."[107]

You will notice that this report never speaks about the acts of violence that this nation and the police departments had long perpetrated against black people. Neither does it talk about the causes that produced the Panthers. It only speaks of the symptoms. In my own lifetime I have experienced and seen the facts as the Panthers have related them.

As some Panthers confessed to stealing and robbing, it was only because they felt that what they took already belonged to them. Their rationale was that the white man had taken it illegally anyway. His long history of exploitation of black people in this country had robbed them of so much that they should have had at birth. They moved with a kind of righteous mood. Individual terror was justified on the basis that it would stop the larger collective terror that had gone on for so long. In some cases, nothing that they could do was so bad that could come close to equalizing the violence this nation was exercising in Vietnam and right here upon black people.

This did not last long; the Panther Parties around the country were raided one by one by the police departments, and many were killed. Those who were not killed were imprisoned. Some left the country and went to live in exile. The

most noted one in exile is Eldridge Cleaver, who joined them and became their most outspoken voice.

The Black Panthers started a mood in the ghettoes of this country that transformed the minds of young blacks in the inner cities into minds of men with race pride and self-respect. They brought about a degree of black consciousness that this country had never seen before. Their program was not one of black supremacy but one of revolution. Yes, one to win the poor people and organize them before the police and the power structure did. Their famous breakfast program was this kind of an effort.

They came at a time when Martin Luther King, Jr., was at the height of his career. They called him a bootlicker.[108] Unlike Martin Luther, the German reformer, King never called upon the state to slaughter the Panthers when they confronted a black exploiter or a white exploiter; he understood the social situation far too well to do that. The peasants of our time had a friend in Martin Luther King, Jr., for that is where he died—in Memphis, Tennessee, with the peasants in their cause.

As we have seen, the reformer and the revolutionist in most cases may desire the same goals. Their proposals for change reflect basically the same ingredients for change with few exceptions—give or take either way. The only difference between the reformer and the revolutionary is how he views change and the methodology he uses to effect it. Their similarities or differences are bound up in what they will do to bring change to pass.

IV

MAN AN INSTRUMENT OF CHANGE AND USER OF INSTRUMENTS OF CHANGE

Constructive changes do not take place by accident or chance. In order for change to take place, there must be a change agent. Someone must have a desire to bring about change. Support must also be available in order to effect change. In other words, a person must have an idea which is different and better than those already present and those that have been presented.

Constructive change is, in most cases, always a slow process. It does not take place overnight. But constructive change takes place within a framework of a recognition of what the problem is and those obstructions which have produced the problem. In addition to a recognition of the problem and its causes, one must have a willingness to consider ways of behaving in relationship to the problem so as to effect change.

Change, then, does not take place within a vacuum, but it takes place in society. It takes place in history, where historical personalities and ideas live and struggle against one another to bring about what they believe to be the best religious or social order. These historical figures become the embodiment of their ideas for change, and these personalities and ideas inevitably come into conflict with those prevailing ideas of the time. So change always comes about as a result of conflict and tension.

AND THE BLACK EXPERIENCE

To talk of change is one thing; to act to bring it about is another thing. Those who would bring about change in society must find ways to actualize their ideas through the process of manifestation. That process, which takes a man from an idea to the actualization of that idea, must include one's behavior in conflict and tension and the use of other instruments available to him.

This chapter, then, is an effort to bring into focus how two individuals, Martin Luther and Martin Luther King, Jr., were instruments of change and how they used other instruments to augment their proposals for change. The chapter also points out the limits of their thought as to a choice of instruments.

Martin Luther, as has been stated previously, recognized the problem of his time. He conceived a way to bring about change based on an understanding of God and man. As Heinz F. MacKenson observed:

Luther believed that the course of history is changed by "great heroes," Wundermanner. The causation of historical change is personal, heroic action by unusual men. Great emperors and conquerors, such as Alexander, Augustus, or Hannibal, philosophers, prophets, and apostles in different ways, forced change upon ordinary men, who would otherwise remain static in their daily routine. God drives on these unusual heroes and uses them to break the cake of custom which inevitably governs the lives of the broad masses. If these heroes recognize God's guidance, they are saved. If they do not, or forget it, their pride will destroy them.[1]

Now, it would be presumptuous to say whether Luther saw himself in the tradition of one of those heroes. However, when we read his explanation of the 101st Psalm there is reason to believe that Luther believed that God endowed certain men with special knowledge and ability to do his will. To this point he says:

Some have a special star before God; these He teaches himself and raises them up as he would have them. They are also the ones who have smooth sailing on earth and so-called good luck and success.

Whatever they undertake prospers; and even if all the world were to work against it, it would still be accomplished without hindrance. For God, who puts it into their heart and stimulates their intelligence and courage, also puts into their hands that it must come to pass and must be carried out; that was the case with Samson, David, Jehoiada, and others. He occasionally provides such men not only among his own people but also among the godless and the heathen; and not only in the ranks of the nobility but also among the middle classes, farmers, and laborers.[2]

Luther did not see man removed from the work of God in the world. Man was here to join God in bringing about his will. But these men, be they great or small, should follow God's direction and give him the praise for their success.[3] The Word of God enabled rulers and others to execute mercy and justice in their dealings with men. What God gave them by way of gifts they were to share with men to effect change. The conflict and the tension enters into play when the evil structures and men appear alongside God's men and their efforts to bring about change. Luther recognizes this:

But so things happen in the world: If God builds a church, the devil comes and builds a chapel beside it, yes, even countless chapels. And so here: If God raises up an outstanding man, either among the spiritual or the secular authorities, the devil brings his monkeys and simpletons to market to imitate everything.[4]

It is important, then, how one reacts to the evil structures which emerge, as this will ultimately determine his effectiveness as a change agent. As has been stated, it is important for the man who would be used by God always to view his task within the confines of God's will for his life. This does not mean to retreat into some isolated place of mystical abode. Luther would never do this because of his belief in the incarnation of God in Christ and what that means for the Christian. Because God was in Christ, we are in Christ and Christ is here in us at work. As Erwin Iserloh put it:

This is a communion in life and destiny, not merely in attitudes. Certainly this shared life with Christ should be actualized in attitudes and deeds, in self-giving on the level of knowing, feeling, and willing.[5]

Martin Luther moved with a knowledge of who he was and who Christ is. He became the imitation of the deeds of Jesus through actualizing his faith in the world. He moved from theory to practice. And he became a practitioner of change first and foremost in his own being, for that was his first legitimate instrument of change. He put his body in jeopardy when it became necessary to witness for the faith.

The best example of the use of being, particularly when it could have meant physical death for Luther, came after his stand at the Diet of Worms. The pope had issued a bull which had in fact given the civil and religious authorities the right to silence Luther from preaching. Further still, as in keeping with the treatment of heretics at the time, it could have meant burning Luther to death if it had been executed. But the Elector Frederick had Luther kidnapped and taken to the Wartburg Castle where he was to stay in seclusion until the situation eased. To the contrary, things did not subside. While the princes chose not to execute the bill against Luther, Carlstadt, Zwilling, and others, the radical wing of the Reformation, had invaded Wittenberg and caused considerable damage and, in Luther's estimation, had perverted the goals of the Reformation in the name of God.

Upon hearing what had happened, Luther in part agreed with some of the changes that had occurred in Wittenberg, but he deplored the ransacking of the churches, the robbery, and the violence. Against the wishes of those who feared for his life, Luther left the safety of Wartburg and journeyed through enemy country to an explosive situation at Wittenberg to preach the gospel. "Melanchthon felt himself helpless in presence of the 'tumult,' declared that no one save Luther himself could quell the excitement, and eagerly pressed his return."[6] Luther, who had grown a beard while at Wartburg,

and had assumed the name "Junker Georg," came to Wittenberg with a sword at his side. It is believed that because he was dressed like a knight no one recognized him in his travel to Wittenberg. In any event, he assessed the situation for two successive days and appeared in the pulpit that Sunday to preach the gospel. For eight days he witnessed with the Lord's Word and with his physical presence. In one of his sermons, he spoke with a sensitive perception and understanding of who he was and who the people were, and thereby decided upon what instruments he would use to fight for his cause:

For the Word created heaven and earth and all things (Psa. 33:6); the Word must do this thing, and not we poor sinners. In short, I will preach it, teach it, write it, but I will constrain no man by force, for faith must come freely without compulsion. Take myself as an example. I opposed indulgences and all the papists, but never with force. I simply taught, preached, and wrote God's Word; otherwise I did nothing. And while I slept [cf. Mark 4:26-29,] or drank Wittenberg beer with my friends Philip and Amsdorf, the Word so greatly weakened the papacy that no prince or emperor ever inflicted such lashes upon it. I did nothing; the Word did everything. Had I desired to foment trouble, I could have brought bloodshed upon Germany; indeed, I could have started such a game that even the emperor would not have been safe. But what would it have been? Mere fool's play. I did nothing; I let the Word do its work. What do you suppose is Satan's thought when one tries to do the thing by kicking up a row? He sits back in Hell and thinks: Oh what a fine game the poor fools are up to now! But when we spread the Word alone and let it alone do the work, that distresses him. For it is almighty and takes captive the hearts, and when the hearts are captured the work will fall of itself.[7]

In this explosive situation, it is important to notice how Luther conducted himself. He does not attack or blame anyone for what has happened at Wittenberg. He sought to calm the people by preaching to them and just by being among them.

Luther took that which he spoke at Wittenberg and that

Word of God which he had translated into the German vernacular and used it to bring about a consciousness and unity in the German people unknown before or since. It was from his seclusion at Wartburg that the new Word came so that the German people could understand the Bible in their language. They could relate to God's Word and see its relevance for their lives. As Gustaf Wingren contends, it was Luther's translation of the Greek word "klesis" to the German word "Beruf" that he denoted a biblical reality.[8] Hence, that reality was to be found in the everyday lives of the sixteenth-century man. It was his vocation and what he was doing—considered as Christian—that helped him to feel equal at least spiritually with the upper classes. The everyday man only needed to discover God's gift to him, his vocation. The ordinary man in Germany, then, saw it in a different way. He no longer needed the pope or the priest to set his boundaries or define for him who he was; the Lord had done it for him. He was equal to all men in God's sight. He was as good in the Christian sense as any priest or monk. Of this language and unity that Luther brought, Goethe was to write: "The Germans became one people through Luther."[9]

With this unity, Luther moved to share with the people a new kind of worship. When the papists attempted to control his reforms, Luther and the German people wrote their own and lived them out in worship. His position was taken always in the name of the gospel. As John H. Tietjen has well stated:

They restored regular preaching to the Mass so that the gospel might be heard. They revised the liturgy of the Mass to eliminate whatever they deemed objectionable to the message of the Gospel. They published hymns and model Sermons and catechetical helps so that people of the Church might come to a renewed appreciation of the Gospel. They placed stress on the sacraments as means by which God conveys His gifts of forgiveness to men.[10]

Martin Luther involved the people in the worship of the

church. Unlike the Roman church, where the priest and the choir did most of the participation, Luther provided means by which the ordinary man as well as the learned man could participate.

Both in his hymns and in his chants he neither disdained the use of older traditional materials nor shrank from revolutionary changes in the interest of German speech rhythm and popular appeal. . . . But it was this basic simplicity and folklike character of Luther's chants that made it possible for the congregation actively to participate in the liturgy.[11]

Martin Luther's use of the hymn helped the German people to sing again in their native tongue. Without any doubt he gave the people, through the instruments he used, a means by which they could relate to the worship of God in the world. In their darkest hour they could sing a hymn, for when the hour of crisis came and life seemed almost meaningless, Luther's great hymn "A Mighty Fortress" was set upon the lips of the ordinary German people. This hymn gathers up Luther's theology and offers inspiration to the struggling souls of the sixteenth century. J. M. Ellison says, "The song then proceeds in Luther's striking imagery to summon all spiritual powers to aid the threatened cause."[12]

But the Reformer is acquainted with the resources of his life. They are grounded in God: for Luther, God was his mighty fortress, his bulwark and his helper in the struggle against all of the satanic forces of those who would keep him and his followers from winning the battle.

So Martin Luther gave to the Germans five great gifts: he gave to the people an example in his being, the Word of God to live by, a language to understand it, a unity to share it, and a worship relevant to their daily life. "A man does not live for himself alone in this mortal body to work for it alone but he lives also for others and not for himself."[13] Martin Luther King, Jr., was a man in whose being dwelled the treasure of the gospel. He was, for black

Americans, God's treasure in an earthen vessel. He was one of those men whom God had endowed with special gifts to effect change. Those of us who knew him felt the warmth of his being and witnessed through our participation the manifestations of some of his ideals and our convictions. King was posited into America's culture as Jesus was posited into the Roman culture. He was among us in a time when the events in this country paralleled those of the Roman Empire in the time of Jesus.

King understood history and systems and how they were used and operated to oppress people—in this case, the Negro and the poor whites. He recognized a problem. That problem for him was not just an individual problem between two people, but it was a problem pervading the collective institutions of a nation. For King, the problem was "Segregation" and "Racism." Evil and sin were realities on every level of man's existence. Speaking of this discovery, he wrote: "Moreover, I came to recognize the complexity of man's social involvement and the glaring reality of collective evil."[14]

As has been stated, most of his education was geared toward finding some means by which to eliminate what he considered the basic evils from the face of the earth. King believed that if evil were to be eradicated, neither man nor God could work alone. But man and God working together could ultimately do the job. This process could never take place without creative and constructive tension. King illumines what he means: "But I must confess that I am not afraid of the word 'tension.' I have earnestly opposed violent tension, but there is a type of constructive, nonviolent tension which is necessary for growth."[15] The kind of tension King was talking about was the kind which brings the issue out in the open where both the nonviolent resister and the oppressor can deal with it. The issue can no longer be ignored in such a tense situation. He further says what he means by constructive tension in his description of nonviolent resistance:

A third characteristic of this method is that the attack is directed against forces of evil rather than against persons who happen to be doing evil. It is the evil that the nonviolent resister seeks to defeat, not the persons victimized by evil. If he is opposing racial injustice, the nonviolent resister has the vision to see that the basic tension is not between races. As I like to say to the people in Montgomery: "The tension in this city is not between white people and Negro people. The tension is, at bottom, between justice and injustice, between the forces of light and the forces of darkness. And if there is a victory, it will be a victory not merely for fifty thousand Negroes, but a victory for justice and the forces of light. We are out to defeat injustice and not white persons who may be unjust."[16]

King was a member of a minority group and he knew that he could not realize his goals or help his people unless he found a practical method by which to do so. King found this method in Mahatma Gandhi's nonviolent resistance. He took that method and combined it with Jesus' philosophy of love and applied it in the quest of black people to win their free entry into the mainstream of American society.

Nonviolent resistance was not so much a philosophy with King, as it was a way of life. His being embodied nonviolent resistance to evil, based on the love ethic of Jesus. As he lived and worked in the movement with this way of life, he matured and his understanding of how it operated.

For King, the nonviolent participant does not exercise the age-old additive "an eye for an eye and a tooth for a tooth," but he absorbs the punishment in the faith that his actions will help to transform the one who inflicts the punishment. This method would relieve the exponent of the philosophy of nonviolence from hating those who were responsible for his oppression. In other words, we could love our enemies and cut off the tragic cycle of hate in the world.

This does not mean that King did not question the problems involved in the application of nonviolent resistance. There were many, for those who were not disciplined in its techniques. So freedom schools were set up before sending

people out to demonstrate. The schools were designed to train them in the techniques of behavior under attack. Though some did not make the transition, for Martin Luther King, Jr., it was his life and weapon in his efforts to bring about change. A classic example of its use is found in one of the many experiences he had during the Montgomery Bus Boycott. This happened at the height of the Movement. He was getting threatening phone calls almost every minute. The police, the mayor, and the KKK had gotten tough; people were criticizing him. As the tension grew, King realized that the threats were real. Fear gripped his heart.

And he found himself wavering in his convictions. Battered by the angry seas of threats, he began to feel it was a real possibility that his life could be snuffed out. Yet, King did not allow himself to be dragged into a state of mind that would have led him to urge retaliation. Even if death came to him, his desire was for all to pursue their quest for equality and dignity in the practice of the nonviolent methods.

Then it all happened, one night in the month of January. He bedded down and began to doze; the telephone rang and another threat was directed against his life. The voice on the other end said, "Listen, nigger, we've taken all we want from you; before next week you'll be sorry you ever came to Montgomery."[17] King hung up the telephone but he could not rest. He was afraid, full of fear, despair, and doubt. This was the most crucial point of his life. On that agonizing night, in the dark chambers of his soul he struggled with himself and God. His fears were too much for him; he met the possibility of physical death head-on. At this point, all of his strength seemed to leave him and he tried to figure out a way to bow graciously out of the Movement without appearing to be a coward.

But as with Jesus in the Garden of Gethsemane, so was it with King. When doubts gripped him, the presence of the Almighty reaffirmed his faith in the cause which he had chosen. He emerged from that experience of fear and doubt a stronger person than before. This was the moment when

King joined the ranks of all of God's men of history who had in deep crises experienced the eternal exemption from the fear of anything.

This was King's Garden of Gethsemane; it was his Wittenberg Tower experience. And soon enough he would get his chance to face that anything-experience. Only three days later his home was bombed. The only reason his family was not killed was that when they heard something hit the porch they moved quickly to another room. King was at a mass meeting when the word of this came. He accepted it with resolution because of his experience a few nights before.

As King journeyed home to see if his wife and child were safe, he noticed the large groups of Negroes gathered. It was a potentially explosive situation. The method of nonviolence as an effective instrument of change was hanging suspended between the angry retaliatory mood of the crowds and upon the contigency of how King would behave. He knew that some of them had weapons and had vowed to have it out with the police and the white community that very night for bombing his home. To the surprise of some and the disappointment of his enemies, that night was King's finest hour. He did not speak in a retaliatory fashion; he merely urged the people to go immediately home and take their weapons; he and his family were all right. His commitment to nonviolence and to the principle of love had again won the day, and he assumed control of the situation. It was from out of his being, of actualizing his faith in a life experience, that Martin Luther King chose the instruments he would use to effect change.

As has been said of Jesus, the same can now be said of Martin Luther King; there he was a member of an oppressed group, and he knew that his dream of the beloved community could not come to pass through violent means. His dream could not be realized within the social order as it existed. Knowing this, King dreamed anyway. He not only dreamed, but he projected that dream beyond the confines of his restrictions in a kind of eschatological language which was

suspended between "what is" and "what ought to be." King's dream always hung between freedom and destiny. He believed that the realization of his dream was possible to some degree in isolated moments of truth and freedom now. I was in the nation's capital on August 28, 1963, when the Word of God for us was given by Martin Luther King. On that day, the Word was directed toward the goal of making the written words of the American creed and those of the Bible become a living experience for all men. He, more than any other man, articulated for us our inarticulate distresses which had accumulated as a result of our long history of oppression and unexpressed feelings and desires. It was as though all of the hopes of the dead unfulfilled blacks came forth in the words of that one man that day. This is the way he spoke:

I say to you today, my friends, that in spite of the difficulties and frustrations of the moment I still have a dream. It is a dream deeply rooted in the American dream.

I have a dream that one day this nation will rise up and live out the true meaning of its creed: "We hold these truths to be self-evident; that all men are created equal."

I have a dream that one day on the red hills of Georgia the sons of former slaves and the sons of former slaveowners will be able to sit down together at the table of brotherhood.

I have a dream that one day even the state of Mississippi, a desert state sweltering with the heat of injustice and oppression, will be transformed into an oasis of freedom and justice.

I have a dream that my four little children will one day live in a nation where they will not be judged by the color of their skin but by the content of their character.

I have a dream today.

I have a dream that one day the state of Alabama, whose governor's lips are presently dripping with the words of interposition and nullification, will be transformed into a situation where little black boys and black girls will be able to join hands with little white boys and white girls and walk together as sisters and brothers.

I have a dream that one day every valley shall be exalted, every hill and mountain shall be made low, the rough places will be

made plains, and the crooked places will be made straight, and the glory of the Lord shall be revealed, and all flesh shall see it together.

This is our hope. This is the faith with which I return to the South. With this faith we will be able to transform the jangling discords of our nation into a beautiful symphony of brotherhood. With faith we will be able to work together, to pray together, to struggle together, to go to jail together, to stand up for freedom together, knowing that we will be free one day.

This will be the day when all of God's children will be able to sing with new meaning "My country 'tis of thee, sweet land of liberty, of thee I sing. Land where my fathers died, land of the pilgrim's pride, from every mountainside, let freedom ring." . . .

When we let freedom ring, when we let it ring from every village and every hamlet, from every state and every city, we will be able to speed up that day when all of God's children, black men and white men, Jews and Gentiles, Protestants and Catholics, will be able to join hands and sing in the words of that old Negro spiritual, "Free at last! Free at last! Thank God Almighty, we are free at last![18]

Martin Luther King not only talked about a dream but he worked across the length and breadth of this nation to make that dream come true. After his success in Montgomery, other areas awaited his presence and the application of the nonviolent approach to the problems of evil. To meet the demands of the hour, Martin Luther King and about one hundred other ministers founded the Southern Christian Leadership Conference. This organization was designed to help eradicate what its founders considered to be the great evils of segregation, discrimination, and oppression from the land. As is the case with all parent organizations, allied groups sprang up elsewhere. This was no less true of the Southern Christian Leadership Conference. With the organization, King took the church out of its cloistered walls into the streets of this nation. As he had used his being and his ability to articulate our case as instruments of change, now with his new organization he could broaden his movement to national application; and it is out of the application of the

technique of nonviolent resistance that we see the emergence of the other instruments which he used—the mass meetings, the marches, and the worship. In this process, a liturgy is developed that brought men together in community. The class levels seemed to fade into the background.

A classic example of this is described in the proceedings of the Montgomery Movement. Here the educated, the non-educated, the middle class, the poverty stricken, the lame, and every other segment of the Negro and white experience was brought together around a common issue: All sang and prayed together. For the false barriers which had kept them apart for so long gave way in the struggle for liberation.

The mass meeting and the marches, whether they were used in Montgomery or in some other city, were always occasions for the creation of new forms of worship and the application of those forms to worship God and do his will in the world.

As King sought to apply his techniques to a situation, there was always a prior assessment before the appeal for direct action and confrontation to evil structures. He shared this approach with us from the Birmingham Movement: "In any nonviolent campaign there are four basic steps: collection of the facts to determine whether injustices exist; negotiation; self-purification; and direct action."[19]

Armed with this knowledge, which he had acquired from the local leaders and his own awareness of the oppression of black people everywhere, King proceeded to a mass meeting to which all local concerned citizens were invited. And it was the mass meeting that brought to birth or revived a liturgy with new meaning for the people. Here all segments of the society met and sang together again. New words were substituted for the old words to suit the time. The new words, however, suited the mood and gathered up the feelings of the people. King was convinced of their effective use:

An important part of the mass meetings was the freedom songs. In a sense the freedom songs are the soul of the movement. They are

more than just incantation of clever phrase designed to invigorate a campaign, they are as old as the history of the Negro in America. They are adaptations of the songs the slaves sang—the sorrow songs, the shouts for joy, the battle hymns and the anthems of our movements. I have heard people talk of their beat and rhythm, but we in the Movement are as inspired by their words. "Woke Up This Morning with My Mind Stayed on Freedom," in a sentence that needs no music to make its point. We sing the freedom songs today for the same reason the slaves sang them, because we too are in bondage and the songs add hope to our determination that "We shall overcome, Black and white together, We shall overcome someday."[20]

These meetings would move from church to church around the given locality so as to include as many people as possible. The black churches were utilized, as well as those black ministers who were as convinced as King was that in the quest for justice and social change no one could stand aloof. As King liked to say: "I am grateful to God that through the influence of the Negro church, the way of non-violence became an integral part of our struggle."[21] Occasionally, there were some black ministers who allowed the white power structure to influence them to believe that King was an outsider. But in such cases, King had his answer because the Southern Christian Leadership Conference had an affiliate in that town or city, and it was at the request of such that he was there. King was there because he firmly believed that, "Injustice anywhere is a threat to justice everywhere. We are caught in an inescapable network of mutuality, tied in a single garment of destiny."[22]

When division occurred within the Negro community and black ministers criticized King, he rose to the occasion with an incisive sharing of his plans and insights as to the role of the preacher and the gospel.

The same was true when the white clergymen drew up their ranks against his actions. He never hesitated to express his disappointment that even they and the white church were on the brink of corrupting the body of Christ.

He did this, however, not without praising those white ministers who had suffered and died for the cause. Writing to answer his white critics from the Birmingham jail cell, he states his case: "Yes, I see the Church as the body of Christ. But, oh! How we have blemished and scarred that body through social neglect and through fear of being nonconformists."[23]

This kind of behavior was rare with King, and this was a distinct difference between his behavior and that of Martin Luther, the German reformer. For King was trying to bring all men together in community, and when he stopped to answer a criticism it was always for the purpose of clarification and toward keeping communications and dialogue going on. This was important to his approach to life. However, if communication and negotiations failed to get results, he was soon to be found back in the streets where he and those who believed as he did were the church witnessing.

It was not so important what King did within the walls of church buildings, but rather it was significant what he did with the authentic faith of the church in the life of Christians in the world. Something happened to him and those who knew him and followed him through participation. It was through participation in the marches, whether they were local or national, that men of all classes and levels and races who would have never met or touched one another were brought together. Here in the march they joined hands and sang songs—the slave songs—and became one in thought and purpose. It was there that the whole question of class faded into the background of the drama.

So like Martin Luther the German reformer, Martin Luther King gave the world his gifts. He gave to the world, and to the black man in particular, an example of the Word of God in his being, the articulation of our inarticulate distressed plight, a new appreciation of who we are, and the resurrection and development of relevant liturgy in the worship of God. He spoke the sentiment of what I am trying to say about him now in a sermon in February, 1968. He spoke

as though he knew that his death was not too far off; he spoke of what he desired to be said of him in the eulogy:

I'd like somebody to mention that day that Martin Luther King, Jr., tried to give his life serving others.

I'd like for somebody to say that day that Martin Luther King, Jr., tried to love somebody.

I want you to say that I tried to be right on the war question. I want you to be able to say that day that I did try to feed the hungry. I want you to say that day that I did try in my life to clothe those who were naked.

I want you to say on that day that I did try in my life to visit those who were in prison. And I want you to say that I tried to love and serve humanity.[24]

Both Martin Luther the German reformer and Martin Luther King knew that in order to bring about change there had to be some social authority. While their thought shows that each man's allegiance was first and foremost to God, they nevertheless respected that temporal authority where it was not oppressive. Their understanding of history and human nature helped them to see that overthrowing one form of tyranny did not necessarily guarantee its replacement by a better form. In fact, there was always the possibility of a more evil structure emerging.

Neither hesitated to criticize the civil authority when he felt it necessary. The difference between the two, however, is that while Martin Luther's criticism was primarily directed against the church, Martin Luther King's criticism was directed toward transforming society, toward demanding that the American nation live up to its constitution. Both knew, therefore, that to live in society people could not exist without some kind of order—an order which set limits on each man's freedom. If change were to come, it had to come within a given context and not in a perpetual state of chaos. So Martin Luther King accepted the penalty for breaking an unjust law. When he did, he voluntarily went to jail to serve his time.

Perhaps that is why the German reformer Martin Luther took the position that God had ordained the state to rule over the temporal order. Luther used the political power of the state when it was advantageous to him. When he felt that the peasants, Muntzer, Carldstadt, and others threatened the fulfillment of his goals, he aligned himself with the state to put them down. And when the church would not call a council to suit his whims, he called upon the princes and the ruling class to do so.

It is out of Martin Luther's understanding of the role that the state was to play in the human affairs of mankind that we find the limits and bounds of his thought, for he firmly believed that the state should have the allegiance of the people in temporal matters.

You ask whether a Christian, also, may bear the secular sword and punish the wicked, since Christ's words, "Thou shalt not resist evil," are so clear and definite that the sophists have had to make council of them. I answer, You have now heard two propositions. The one is, that the sword can have no place among Christians, therefore you cannot bear it among and against Christians, who do not need it. The question, therefore, must be directed to the other side, to the non-Christian, whether as a Christian you may there bear it. Here the other proposition applies, that you are under obligation to serve and further the sword by whatever means you can, with body, soul, honor or goods. For it is nothing that you need, but something quite useful and profitable for the whole world and for your neighbor. Therefore, should you see that there is a lack of hangmen, beadles, judges, lords, or princes, and find that you are qualified, you should offer your services and seek the place, that necessary government may by no means be despised and become inefficient or perish. For the world cannot and dare not dispense with it.[25]

Here Luther all but said that where violence is necessary it is the duty of the state to administer it and never the Christian. It appears that Luther condones the use of violence as long as it is done by the state. He did not offer any alternative to killing. Here his thought is limited and his-

tory has proven it in the doings of Hitler. Luther's irrational statements against the peasants and also against the Jews gave the Hitler regime the language and what it considered to be a righteous reason for killing. His possible overemphasis on faith alone in some sense contributed to the Church's lethargy in not opposing Hitler more vigorously. As William L. Shirer observed:

It is difficult to understand the behavior of most German Protestants in the first Nazi years unless one is aware of two things: their history and the influence of Martin Luther. The great founder of Protestantism was both a passionate anti-Semite and a ferocious believer in absolute obedience to political authority. He wanted Germany rid of the Jews and when they were sent away he advised that they be deprived of "All their cash and jewels and silver and gold" and; furthermore, "that their synagogues or schools be set on fire, that their houses be broken up and destroyed . . . and they be under a roof or stable, like the gypsies . . . in misery and captivity as they incessantly lament and complain to God about us"—advice that was followed four centuries later by Hitler, Goering and Himmler.[26]

John Warwick Montgomery accuses Shirer of reviving the thesis held by Peter F. Wiener in his *Martin Luther: Hitler's Spiritual Ancestor* and not being true to Luther's writings on the issue at hand.[27] Despite what Montgomery or anyone else says, it can never be ruled out that Luther's abusive statements and uncontrolled behavior in some of the crises of his life furnished those who would not or could not understand his theology as a whole, with the fuel necessary to fan the flames of hate and killing. Furthermore anyone who cannot understand Martin Luther's doctrine of salvation by faith alone could see how those of the German church could find in it a rationale for sitting back and waiting for God to do what they should have done. With few exceptions—Karl Barth, Niemoller, Bonhoeffer, and a few others—the church acquiesced to the Hitler regime.

Martin Luther King, on the other hand, was more care-

ful in the language he used and the behavior he exemplified in crisis situations. When people attacked him, he never spoke in a retaliatory fashion. When the black power slogan emerged and challenged his position, he attempted to counsel his brothers with understanding. Martin Luther King understood what produced the Panthers and the Stokeley Carmichaels and the Rap Browns. When the government and the moderates called upon him to repudiate the Panthers, he did not call for their annihilation. He responded by calling attention to the causes that produced such human behavior. His language could never be used as justification for killing. On the other hand, those who did not understand his philosophy could read into it a call to death in the sense of a martyr movement. His life and action leave that possibility open. To me, that could be a weakness for those who do not understand him.

John Oliver Killens makes a striking observation of the possible weakness of Martin Luther King's method of nonviolence as being useful in some situations. But he further observes:

The Problem is the tendency to take such a tactic and build it into a way of life, the growing tendency to invalidate all other tactics, as if the tactic of nonviolence were the only road to freedom. But the truth of the matter is there are many highways and byways and depending on the circumstances every single one must be traveled.[28]

As Killens has said, that is exactly what Martin Luther King did. He made of nonviolent resistance a way of life and sought to get others to accept it. This negated the whole right of self-defense and the freedom to bear arms. But, all men are not willing to do what Martin Luther King was able to do; and they will never be willing or able to in this country with its past and present history of violence. Ultimately, Martin Luther King's solution is correct, though its practical application may be difficult for the almost thirty million blacks in this country.

When Gandhi used this technique in India to free her from the yoke of British colonialism, the Indians were in the majority; it seems to me that this is what made the difference. Here in America it is difficult to believe that the majority would hesitate to wipe blacks out if they revolted in the fashion of Nat Turner or in an intensified militant nonviolence of Martin Luther King. In the human affairs of men and nations, power is very seldom shared as it ought; it must be taken, as it is never given.

Perhaps if there is any criticism that could be leveled at Martin Luther King, it would be his inability to include the Stokeley Carmichaels fully in his movement. Martin Luther King was concerned with bringing people together, regardless of race, creed, or color. He was firmly convinced that there was enough goodness in man to respond to unmerited suffering. He did not see why it was necessary to move from alliances with whites for tactical reasons. The truth of the matter is that the term black power, King feared, would alienate the white friends from the movement. To some degree, he equated black power with black supremacy or with white power. But black power cannot by any stroke of the imagination be equated with white power, either economically, politically, or any other way. On the Meredith, Mississippi, Freedom March, King could have embraced blackness more fully and used blackness as a positive instrument of change, thus bringing young people into the Movement as never before.

Yet, in a strange way, Martin Luther King understood what was happening in the black community. He felt it himself. He understood the growing frustrations and anger. Still he could never bring himself to take up any weapon other than love to fight his cause. He, perhaps, cut off that possibility because he came close to, if not actually to, the point of making nonviolent resistance an absolute. He believed that love at the center of life could transform the oppressor. But love ought to be reciprocal. As Hans Walton, Jr., put it: "Love, it would seem, needs not only to be given voluntarily,

but needs also to be a two-way process if it is to transform human relations."[29]

It would indeed have been a benefit to all of us to have been able to observe Martin Luther King longer in terms of his behavior in the hour of crisis, particularly had he lived to face this nation head-on with his Poor Peoples' Campaign. That was the first time he really proposed some hard solutions for the nation to act out in providing a decent life for its poor. It was the first time—had he been successful in bringing it to pass—that real benefits would have reached down to the poor man. To that point, the people who had benefited most from his efforts, by and large, were the middle-class Negroes.

In our quest to surmise what his behavior would have been had he lived to see the war continued in Vietnam and the continued violence perpetrated upon the black man, we may study his last published statement:

I am not sad that Black Americans are rebelling: this was not only inevitable but eminently desirable. Without this magnificent ferment among Negroes, the old evasions and procrastinations would have continued indefinitely. Black men have slammed the door shut on the past of deadening passivity. Except for the Reconstruction years, they have never in their long history on American soil struggled with such creativity and courage for their freedom. These are our bright years of emergence; though they are painful ones, they cannot be avoided.[30]

V

A PRELUDE TO THE UNFINISHED REFORMATION

The Reformer Martin Luther began what has become known as the Protestant Reformation. His reactions were against a variety of secular, man-made abuses of the word of God inculcated in the practices of the Roman Catholic Church. Luther was not a revolutionary, but at heart a Reformer. He sought to return to the truth of the past, not to destroy the organization of the present. He refused to live with lies and injustices perpetuated by the church, but went back and reclaimed the heritage which he had been forced to give up when he became an Augustinian monk, a priest and subsequently, a theologian.

In many ways philosophical as well as by name, Martin Luther King, Jr. echoed his thoughts, inner turmoil, and struggle with the system. He was not a revolutionary, like Luther, he insisted on reclaiming the freedoms, rights, and privileges which had been stolen from him and all black people when they first arrived on these shores in the slave ships. Just as Martin Luther had to deal with his more rebellious brethren during the Peasants Revolt, so did King with the Black Panthers and non-violent militant groups.

It seems appropriate at this point to reflect upon the meanings and methods of these two religious giants for our time. Both Martin Luther and Martin Luther King, Jr. lived and worked toward a better day for their people. We may not agree with all that they did to alleviate the plagues of oppressive men and unjust institutions, yet, we are challenged to

take notice of those areas which are common to the quest of all human beings. Indeed, this is what is ultimately important for man's pilgrimage on earth.

First and foremost in the struggle of each man is the quest for authentic identity. What I speak of here is identity in the sense that one is able to search for his or her true self-hood and not that which is arbitrarily imposed upon the person or group by some outside force, institution, or group. Furthermore, once the individual has searched and found the true personhood of his own being, he should then be able, without hindrance, to live and work out that vision under God. This of course, involves ones awareness and understanding of what he is to do in the world in accord with what he perceives to be the will of God for his life.

The facts of history and of human experience have disclosed what Martin Luther and Martin Luther King, Jr. viewed as the priorities for their lives. Each man goes through an intellectual quest in order to get at how he will deal with the problems of his day. This process aided them in resolving in their own minds what solutions would be offered. At the same time, however, they are burdened with forces from within and without with which they do not accept nor agree. Martin Luther is haunted by the justice of God and his inability to satisfy Him with good works, though he had tried. His sense of sinfulness remains until he stumbles upon a new discovery after studying Paul's letter to the Romans. This initial struggle in Luther is complicated by an institution and its leaders who insist to a large extent, he can win his way to heaven by doing good works. Martin Luther, of course, knows after much striving that what they claim and advocate is impossible for him. He finds his answer in Romans 1:17, "He who through faith is righteous shall live." This was a liberating moment for Luther. It set him free to pursue his life's work in a new way with an assurance he had not known before. The shame he once felt fell off like broken chains. He was free to live as an authentic human being. Neither the institution to which he belonged and loved nor its leaders were any longer off limits for him to propose reforms and other criticisms. Those proposals have been delineated and the methods Luther used to implement them. Martin Luther

King, however, is motivated by his own sense of fair play and his understanding of the gospel of Christ and his exposure to Mahatma Ghandi. After having heard Dr. Mordecai Johnson speak with such fervor and admiration about Ghandi and the success he had achieved in winning the independence of India from under the yoke of British colonialism, King felt that Ghandi's principles could be applied to the conditions of Black people here in America. Coupled with this awareness King also added the New Testament concept of the beloved community. It is amazingly clear how King used the Ghandian concept of Satyagrapha along with Jesus' ethic of love to implement his reforms for our times. This Ghandian concept had the same impact upon the mind and life of Martin Luther King as Paul's letter to the Romans had upon the mind and life of Martin Luther. It became King's vehicle upon which to hang his methods of reforms. His wife, Corretta, described for us an example of the obvious similarity between her Martin and Martin Luther of the sixteenth century.

Martin was prepared, and in a magnificent symbolic gesture that rang down the centuries from his namesake, he nailed his demands to the closed door of City Hall, as Martin Luther had nailed his Ninety-Five Theses to the door of Wittenburg.[1]

The above reference took place in Martin Luther King, Jr.'s Chicago campaign, where he confronted the civil authorities to relinquish the liberties that the Constitution of the United States allowed for it's citizens. His bold efforts in the South and the North has challenged us to reflect upon what we must do now.

In addition to their discovery of authentic identity in accord with the will of God, both men believed and lived an incarnational theology. To each man words alone were always cheap commodities that could be peddled by even the devil's simpletons. The difference, however, between evil men and men of God was disclosed in the way one allowed himself to be used by God. God's man always viewed what he did within the confines of God's will for his life. Communion with life and destiny is not merely found in attitudes or in some mystical isolated retreat apart from the real world. It is man's and woman's capacity to live a shared life with Christ; one actualized in not only pious pronouncements, but rather in deeds

and human feelings. We must join God wherever he is at work in His world in the midst of people. This further means putting your money where your words have been. It further means putting your bodies where the action is. Martin Luther did so at the Diet of Worms and in the City of Wittenburg. Martin Luther King, Jr. did it at Montgomery and in Memphis. Both men knew all too well that the word without flesh became a moribund cliché.

The third aspect of Martin Luther and Martin Luther King, Jr. is found in what each man was able to do in order to interpret their respective struggle in understandable terms to the common man. Without the involvement of the large masses of common folk the Reformation Movement and the Civil Rights Movement would have failed. When Martin Luther translated the Bible into the German vernacular, he gave the common man the word so that he could read it for himself. He shined the light of truth upon the Roman Catholic hierarchy in such a way that the common man could see the discrepancies in relation to what the Scriptures held. The availability of the word of God to the masses became their greatest weapon against the distortions of the Papacy and his supporters.

Like Luther before him Martin Luther King, Jr. also gave to the masses a new way of looking at the original documents upon which this country was founded. The Bill of Rights, the Declaration of Independence, and the Constitution of the United States had been grossly misrepresented by the leaders of this nation. He felt that America had become schizophrenic in her behavior. She spoke one way but lived another way when it came to dealing with the minorities and the poor; especially those who were Black. He then made available to the common man an unusual amount of material by which he came to see the racism and the horrors of a segregated society. If it was unfair in Martin Luther's sixteenth century Europe for the Nobles and the priest to fleece the peasants, it was surely unfair in Martin Luther King, Jr's. twentieth century world for the rich nations to get richer and the poor to get poorer.

To put it bluntly, both Martin Luther and Martin Luther King, Jr. shared a common concern for the need to treat all human beings with dignity and equality. That mandate had

been a strong tradition among the early Hebrew and Christian people of the earth. Both men felt it should be continued in their times. Martin Luther demonstrated his concern for this tradition through the ways in which he lived among the common people of Germany and his willingness to make available to them in their own culture and tongues what he knew and possessed for himself. The same potentials which had been developed in him should be made available to every man and woman, whatever their respective vocations. This is why he sought to elevate the common man's vocation to the same level the clergy shared. To Martin Luther all honest work was sacred and should be treated in a meaningful way. Martin Luther King, Jr. in a comparable way did the same thing for his time. He spoke out against the war machines of our Military Industrial Complex for the way they were destroying the resources, and people of poorer nations of the earth.

Martin Luther was called a heretic by the Roman Catholic hierarchy and Martin Luther King, Jr. was called unpatriotic and a Communist by the perpetrators of social injustices. Nevertheless, they both held forth toward their very difficult tasks in their times, and by the power of God faced them.

Having reflected upon some of the important similarities between Martin Luther and Martin Luther King, Jr., it seems appropriate now to focus toward several affirmations for the future. As there were oppressive institutions in the sixteenth century to which Martin Luther spoke, there are structures and issues, which are present in our times that need to be addressed. As has been stated, Martin Luther's struggle was with the Roman Catholic hierarchy. Martin Luther King's efforts were directed against the walls of segregation and racism. In the thought and life of both men there are foundations for our struggles ahead.

Several of these ideas can serve to strengthen our efforts to address the issues and evils of our day. However, we will be unable to move with a positive and constructive stance unless we learn to affirm the truth about what has happened between us, both Black and White. There is still a shame and fear which hangs like a crippling chain rendering Black Folks unable to develop their potentials. It is born of a long history

of psychological, economic, social and religious misinformation. Furthermore, this stripping process has left many, far too many with a feeling of inferiority. In other words, to my dismay, many Blacks still feel that they are not as good as some other people on this earth. This is a concocted myth; a racist coinage. There is no truth to it; none at all. Martin Luther King, Jr. gave his whole life to show us all, both Black and White that it was a lie.

Before one can offer a healthy solution to the problems involved in the Black Experience, the major premise that the Church must reassert itself as the vehicle to transport Black people from humiliation to a destination called *the beloved community.* In his book *The Black Church: Relevant or Irrelevant in the 21st Century*, Reginald F. Davis believes there is a crisis in Black America in particular. Disproportionately, Blacks rank at the top of many sociological indicators that are pathological in nature. Slavery is over, yet many Blacks are not healed, organized nor liberated. The relevant church corrects oppression rather than maintain it. An irrelevant church sees the self-destructive behavior of people and refuses to take the necessary steps to eradicate it. The White Church cannot be silent on correcting the issues of racism but must be involved as agents of change to bring justice and liberation to all. Ultimately, the Church (Black and White) must come together to be the Word of God to the poor, the oppressed and the marginalized.

The story of the Black Church's pilgrimage in North America has been one of fusion, adaptation, survival and protest. The fusion of our African religious practices and those of the Christian religion has led us from the invisible brush arbor experience to the visible institutional church. In the almost four hundred years since we first put feet upon the shores of America we have become Baptist, African Methodist Episcopal, African Methodist Episcopal Zion, Christian Methodist Episcopal, Black Pentecostals, (Church of God and Christ), other Holiness groups, Black Israelites (Jews), Black Muslims, Christian Centers,

and the latest of which is the Full Gospel Movement. In addition to the abovementioned denominations, there are others who remain within some of the larger white communions such as the United Methodist, the Protestant Episcopal, Presbyterian, Lutheran's, and Roman Catholic churches. Add to these the new and emerging interest by young black males in Louis Farrakhan and the Black Muslims highlighted by the 1996 Million-Man March, to a degree the 2000 Million Family March and a fuller religious picture will evolve.

In reading the stellar history of some of the larger Black denominations, their accomplishments on behalf of the African American community and the nation could cause one to speculate that the future of Black religious life would be at least as bright as its past. Such speculation may be premature. While the Black Church is still vibrant and maintaining its membership, there are some crucial issues with which we must deal. Among these are race, fragmentation within the Black Church, the role of women in the life of the church, the church's response to welfare reform, economic empowerment, the healing and restoration of the black family, the dismantling of white images, and psychological renovations. One other consideration of extreme importance is the threat of assimilation or absorption into white groups. The emergence of personalities like Rick Warren, Joel Osteen, Randy Gilbert, Rod Parsley and now Jonathan Falwell leave many black parishioners engaged in escapism from the pain of the black church and finding a haven of peace or an antidote in the vastness of the white mega church movement.

Let me say just a few words about race. As I look back, over the last fifty years, I am proud of the progress we have made in the area of racial understanding. However, we still have a long way to go. What happened to Martin Luther Kings' Dream for America? His dream was certainly not the continuation of more rigid clandestine racist practices by the dominate culture. His dream projected a society in which the Constitution's promises

would be realized, and want would cease. There would be plenty for all in the redistribution of wealth in America. At one time, we thought that racial problems were only prevalent in the South, only to learn that they were in Boston, Chicago, New York, Newark, Watts, and other cities. It still pervades our American culture: North, South, East and West.

The rise of Black Nationalism and Black Power sent liberal whites, who thought that they were saviors of African Americans, running for cover. It also embarrassed conservative African Americans, because they could not explain, to their so-called liberal friends, what was going on and why. They did not discern or understand that freedom was being actualized in young Black people. To be free meant to be all they could be under God unencumbered by the restrictions of white society. While this behavior frightened liberal whites and embarrassed conservative Blacks, it pleased conservative whites and provided them with reasons for the resegregation of American society.

Even though Republican, John McCain on November 5, 2008 conceded to Democrat Barack Obama, the son of a father from Kenya and the first Black President of the United States, conservative whites and blacks through political groups like the Tea Party have not conceded ongoing efforts to label liberal articulate blacks as socialists. Therefore, Obama and his followers (Obama zombies) are the cause of America's problems rather than repairers of the persisting problems of our time. The actions of the Tea Party with chagrin reminds us that those who hoped Kings' dream was fulfilled and made incarnate through the singular event of the Obama election and occupancy of 1600 Pennsylvania Avenue (White House) are left still hoping and the dream yet deferred. Tavis Smiley through the series of works around The Covenant and others are seeking to suggest solutions to the demises of the King's dream that if for only a moment we thought would be made incarnate through the singular event of the Obama election and his African American family in the White House.

Secondly, let me say a word about the fragmentation we are experiencing from within. In time past, we could readily identify the external enemies: namely racism, segregation, and the lack of access to the basic benefits of American society. Presently, Black denominations are under attack from within. Attacks such as the impact of a paradigm shift away from the practice of a support-ive community to a threatening stance of individualism. In other words, from the mid-nineteenth century to the post World War II Period, Black denominations were comprised of persons with a mindset that believed in supporting the institutions of family, church and schools; these were good for the community. Some individuals are now leading churches that think the "notion" that if some-thing is not in it for personal gain, then they will not be supportive. The issues concerning women, gays, lesbians, the full gospel movement and the disparity between the black middle class and the black underclass unduly propel this par-adigm shift. Excessive emphasis upon the above tend to cause our resources to be diminished and breeds fragmentation.

A third concern is the direction in which some in the Black Churches are moving. An inquiry into the local black religious and national denominations will yield little, if any, movement from the white denominations to the black denom-inations. On the other hand, evidence can be found where some blacks are moving toward white denominations and becoming a part of them.

As efforts to assimilate into the larger culture increases, blacks are adapting white fundamentalist and conservative theologies, which do not address the needs of the black com-munity. These theologies tend to focus more on getting saved and shallow morality as prerequisites for salvation. Some of these groups have vast machinery of money-raising tech-niques that blanket the world to support individualistic con-cerns of independent mega church movements. Much of this is showcased through the medium of television and the print-ed literature. To what extent these influences will have on black congregants remained to be seen.

A fourth issue is the role of women in the black denomination. This is a fact often ignored. The majority of members in African American congregations are women. With regard to their roles, present positions include Christian Educators, associate, and assistant pastors. Exceptions to these would be found in some of the Pentecostal and Methodist churches. In these institutions, women are given leadership positions just as men. However, in far too many of our Baptist and some other churches, the place of leadership is reserved for males only. To make matters worse, the National Baptist Convention, U.S.A., Inc., on August 24, 1998 received a report from a committee on Constitutional revisions which stated: "Resolved that the New Testament only addresses Ordination of persons of the masculine gender. It is the position of this convention (National Baptist Convention U.S.A. Inc.,) to maintain our present stance with the New Testament teachings."[2] Thank God that this did not become official practice. What is troubling about this statement is the fact that at this late date in our history a large group of us are still insisting on gender exclusivity. The relevant question for the future is "To what extent will the black churches invite women to lead as they do men?" Regarding women in a broader sense, this writer applauds the efforts of local pastors and activists who protest the use of misogynistic language in lyrics on BET and the rap industry. This is a clear example of the Church reasserting itself on the critical matter of the portrayal of black women in society.

The fifth and sixth crucibles are that the church's response to welfare reform and economic empowerment can be combined. Since there are thousands, if not millions, who are now federally subsidized, concrete programs that will sustain these individuals and their families while they are prepared for the job market, must be put in place. It seems prudent that the black denominations and other agencies, such as philanthropic organizations, could team up in a cooperative venture with the federal government. This would help to salvage the lives and futures of those who have been handicapped by their long dependence

upon the welfare system. When emancipation came to the African Americans in 1865, a similar program under the direction of the Freedman's Bureau was established to assist men, women, and children in coping with life without the supervision of the plantation.

Self-help ideology was propagated through the black church and also though the education offered in the Black schools and colleges which had been founded. These schools offered skills in brick masonry, carpentry, plastering, plumbing, electricity, and made jobs available. At that time, the black population needed to build not only institutions but also individual homes. In former days, blacks built not only institutions but also individual homes. In former days, blacks built their churches, schools, homes and places of business. What I am suggesting may seem far-fetched, but if we are really serious about moving people from welfare to be self-sustaining, employment and home ownership must go hand and hand. There is a definite need for the Church to reassert itself in welfare reform through pointing to the model of the first century Church despite the urging of the Tea Party that those that preach the social gospel are advocates of socialism. Economic empowerment efforts such as credit unions and practical teachings provided to blacks regarding how our Economic system works are critical to combat Carter G. Woodson's notion of the mis-education of the Negro or the non existence of education in this foundational area necessary for self-sufficiency.

Finally, the healing and restoration of the black family has to become a priority. The model for such a venture could very well be based upon the African proverb; "It takes a village to raise a child." Where many in my generation grew up, this proverb was the standard by which we were nurtured into adulthood. The home, the school, the church, and the total community took responsibility for the way we behaved. When we committed an act of evil against the interest of the community, we were reprimanded, forgiven, and restored.

MARTIN LUTHER–MARTIN LUTHER KING, JR.
AND THE BLACK EXPERIENCE

We need to return to the early African American family models that are in our distant pasts. These models were informed by the Bible, which recognizes the extended family in which the community plays a vital role in nurturing and shaping the individuals.

The aforementioned issues must be addressed with imagination and creativity. If black denominations fail to do so, the church may not remain the church, which has served as a corrective of the dominant culture, and has traditionally sought to meet the needs of black people.

The call to African Americans to remember the models inherent within our culture need to be a clear call in order that all who have ears may hear. This summons need not be subdued by remorse over the lost good behind us nor by fear of the unknown possibilities that lie ahead of us.

The fragmentation which we are experiencing need not continue as a norm for those who feel left out by their differences and those who seek affirmation and acceptance within our communions. At one time, the church was the only place where African Americans could go to feel a sense of oneness and a sense of belonging. This was true for both the rural and the urban churches.

Therefore, our invitation should go forth to the lesbians, the gays, those with aids, women who seek leadership roles, the middle class, the underclass, and those who are considered by some, to be undesirable. This is the church that I long to experience and to know; where all of God's children can worship, where the strong will help to bear the burdens of the weak and where the whole community seeks to empower all.

We must continue as Martin Luther King, Jr. would continue were he here with us. The church would be an excellent place to foster the kind of programs that can help all people to affirm their true identity under God and dispel the shame.

Programs that I offer at this period in our history are not new nor are they given with any great detailed analysis. That will come at some future time I hope. What I want to suggest in these few remaining words are some few hints as to the shape such ideas may take.

This would involve the dismantling of all the pictures and images in our churches, which depict the deity and the Saints

of the church as being only of the white race. The facts of history confirm to us that the Saints were both Black and white. Henceforth, if their pictures or images are to be painted or sculptured they should be done in such a way as to reflect the same. As one brother put it to me one day, "Why must I always see Jesus as a white man in art?" He need not always see the deity in such presentations. The time has come as Countee Cullen put it a long time ago, to look at Jesus Christ as <u>The Black Christ.</u> He reflects our sufferings and strivings as he reflects those of all races that make up the human family.

To speak of psychological renovations is not enough to help lift our people from out of the pits of shame and deprivation. We must begin to deal successfully with economic schemes that will equip people to live with as much dignity as is possible in a capitalistic society. This process will take both a commitment from the Religious communities, the national governments, the states, and the local municipalities of our land. This is what Martin Luther and Martin Luther King, Jr. would have supported.

A concluding word by way of a true story goes as follows: "As a lad growing up in the country, I experienced some wonderful models of what it means to be community and to be empowered. At the time most farmers needed to have barns built, corn shucked at harvest, peanuts popped and assistance in the slaughter of hogs. The way this was done illustrates more than I can say in words what it means to empower and include persons. The seasons for these tasks necessitated our coming together for the women to cook a common meal and the men to perform the different labors. At the end of a barn raising, hog killing, corn shucking, or peanut popping, no one was too physically spent, for all shared in the processes. At the appointed time, all of the laborers were summoned around a common table to a common meal, to eat and fellowship and then return to their respective homes." This was teamwork; in unity there is always strength; and all are empowered.

NOTES

1. *The Random House Dictionary of The English Language,* ed. by Laurence Urdany (New York: Random House, 1966), s.v. "experience."

2. Alfred Lord Tennyson, *Ulysses,* in *Representative Poems,* ed. by Samuel C. Chew (New York: The Odyssey Press, 1941), p. 58.

3. Roland H. Bainton, *Here I Stand* (New York: Abingdon, 1951), p. 21, (hereinafter cited as *Here I Stand*).

4. E. G. Schwiebert, *Luther and His Times* (Saint Louis: Concordia Publishing House, 1950), p. 109. (hereinafter cited as *Luther and His Times*).

5. Ibid., p. 109.

6. A. C. McGiffert, *Martin Luther: His Life and His Work* (New York: The Century Company, 1911), p. 8 (citing Luther, but does not indicate source or page number).

7. Allan W. Townsend, *A Short Life of Luther* (Philadelphia: Fortress Press, 1967), pp. 18–19.

8. Joanne Grant, ed., *Black Protest: History, Documents, and Analyses 1619 To The Present* (Greenwich, CT: A Fawcett Premier Book, 1968), p. 7.

9. W. E. B. Du Bois, *The World of Africa* (New York: The Viking Press, 1947), p. 80.

Chapter II

1. Martin Luther, *Sermons on The Gospel of St. John,* trans. by Martin H.

Bertram, Vol. XXIII of *Luther's Works,* ed. Jaroslav Pelikan (Saint Louis: Concordia Publishing House, 1959), p. 58 (hereinafter cited as *Sermons on St. John,* 23).

2. Earnest De Witt Burton, *A Critical and Exegtical Commentary on the Epistle to The Galatians* (New York: Charles Scribner's Sons, 1950), p. 460.

3. Ibid., p. 461.

4. Ibid.

5. Ibid., p. 468.

6. William F. Arndt and F. Wilbur Gingrich, *A Greek English Lexicon of The New Testament and Other Early Christian Literature* (Chicago: The University of Chicago Press, 1963), p. 196.

7. Ibid.

8. Ibid.

9. Augustine, *The Spirit and the Letter,* trans. by John Burnaby, Vol. VIII of *Library of Christian Classics,* editors, John Baillie and others, 26 vols. (Philadelphia: The Westminster Press, 1953–66), 205 (hereinafter cited as Augustine, *Spirit and the Letter,* 8).

10. Ibid., p. 205.

11. Ibid., p. 208.

12. Uras Saarnivaara, *Luther Discovers The Gospel* (Saint Louis: Concordia Publishing House, 1951), p. 14.

13. Martin Luther, *Lectures on Romans,* trans. by Wilheim Pauck, Vol. XV of *Library of Christian Classics,* editors John Baillie and others. (Philadelphia: The Westminster Press, 1961), 15: xxxvi.

14. Martin Luther, *Psalm LI,* trans. and ed. by Jaroslav Pelikan, Vol. XII of *Luther's Works* (Saint Louis: Concordia Publishing House, 1959), 12:313.

15. Martin Luther, *Preface to Latin Writings,* in *Selected Writings of Martin Luther,* trans. by Lewis W. Spitz, Sr., and ed. by Theodore G. Tappert (Philadelphia: Fortress Press, 1967) pp. 26–27.

16. Augustine, *The Spirit and the Letter,* p. 205.

17. Martin Luther, *Ninety-Five Theses,* trans. by C. M. Jacobs and revised by Harold J. Grim, Vol. XXXI of *Luther's Works,* ed. by Helmut T. Lehmann (Philadelphia: Munlenberg Press, 1957), 28 (hereinafter cited as *Ninety-Five Theses* 31).

Notes

18. Martin Luther, *The Argument of St. Paul's To The Galatians*, trans. and ed. by Jaroslav Pelikan, Vol. XXVI of *Luther's Works* (Saint Louis: Concordia Publishing House, 1963), 26:5.

19. Ibid., p. 6.

20. Martin Luther, *Letter to George Spenlein*, trans. and ed. by Gottfried G. Krodel, Vol. XLVIII of *Luther's Works* (Philadelphia: Concordia Publishing House, 1963), 48:12.

21. Martin Luther, *Sermon on St. Thomas' Day, Psalm 19:1*, trans. and ed. by John W. Doberstein, Vol. LI of *Luther's Works* (Philadelphia: Muhlenberg Press, 1959), 51:19.

22. Martin Luther, *The Freedom of A Christian*, ed. by John Dillenberger, in *Martin Luther: Selections From His Writings* (New York: Anchor Books, 1961), p. 60 (hereinafter cited as *Selections From His Writings*.)

23. *Sermons on St. John*, 23:58.

24. *Selections From His Writings*, p. 501.

25. Ibid.

26. Martin Luther, *The Disputation Concerning Justification*, trans. by Lewis W. Spitz, Vol. XXXIV of *Luther's Works*, ed. by Helmut T. Lehmann (Philadelphia: Muhlenberg press, 1960), 34:151.

27. Martin Luther, *Theses Concerning Faith and Law*, trans. by Lewis W. Spitz, Vol. XXXIV of *Luther's Works*, ed. by Helmut T. Lehmann (Philadelphia: Muhlenberg Press, 1960), 34:111.

28. *Sermons of Martin Luther* (Philadelphia: Desilver Thomas and Company, 1835), p. 30 (hereinafter cited as *Sermons of Martin Luther*.)

29. *Sermons of Martin Luther*, p. 30.

30. *Selections From His Writings*, p. 70.

31. Ibid., p. 116.

32. Stewart W. Herman, *The Rebirth of the German Church* (New York: Harper and Brothers Publishers, 1946), p. 31.

33. Benjamin Quarles, *The Negro in the Making of America* (New York: The Macmillan Company, 1968), pp. 28–29.

34. Kenneth M. Stampp, *The Peculiar Institution* (New York: Alfred A. Knopf, 1956), p. 12.

35. Lerone Bennett, Jr., *Before the Mayflower* (Baltimore: Penguin Books, 1966), p. 45, citing Charles S. Johnson. (I am assuming that this was cited from Charles S. Johnson's *Shadow of The Plantation.* Bennett does not indicate the specific source or page. Hereinafter' cited as *Before the Mayflower.*)

36. Quarles, *The Negro in the Making of America*, pp. 69–70.

37. E. Franklin Frazier, *The Negro Family in the United States* (Chicago: The University of Chicago Press, 1966), p. 28, citing Robert Anderson, *From Slavery to Affluence:* Memoirs of Robert Anderson, Ex-Slave, p. 19.

38. Ibid., p. 18.

39. Bennett, *Before the Mayflower*, p. 84.

40. W. J. Cash, *The Mind of the South* (New York: Alfred A. Knopf, Inc., 1941), p. 87.

41. Melville J. Herskovits, *The American Negro* (Bloomington, IN: Indiana University Press, 1964), p. 10.

42. E. Franklin Frazier, *The Negro Church in America* (New York: Shocken Books, 1963), p. 4 (hereinafter cited as *The Negro Church in America.*)

43. Frazier, *The Negro Church in America*, p. 5, citing Lorenzo D. Turner, *Africanisms in the Gullah Dialect,* p. 40.

44. John Hope Franklin, *From Slavery to Freedom* (New York: Alfred A. Knopf, 1956), p. 40.

45. Quarles, *The Negro in the Making of America*, p. 71.

46. Ibid.

47. Gunnar Myrdal, *An American Dilemma*, 2 vols. (New York: McGraw-Hill Book Company, 1964), p. 220.

48. Ibid., p. 443, citing William Summer Jenkins, *Pro-Slavery Thought in the Old South,* p. 286

49. Ibid., p. 223.

50. James Weldon Johnson and J. Rosamond Johnson, *The Book of American Negro Spirituals* (New York: The Viking Press, 1925), p. 17.

51. Sterling A. Brown, Arthur P. Davis, and Ulysses Lee, eds., *The Negro Caravan* (New York: Arno Press and The New York Times Press, 1970), p. 413.

52. Sterling Brown, "Negro Folk Expression: Spirituals, Seculars, Ballads and Work Songs," in *The Making of Black America,* August Meier and Elliott Rudwick, eds. (New York: Antheneum, 1969), p. 213.

53. Benjamin E. Mays, *The Negro's God: As Reflected in His Literature* (New York: Antheneum, 1968), pp. 28–29 (hereinafter cited as *The Negro's God.*)

54. John Hope Franklin, "The Bitter Years of Slavery," *Life,* 65 (November, 1968): 112.

55. Frederick Douglass, *Life and Times of Frederick Douglass* (New York: The Citadel Press, 1953), p. 66.

56. Miles Mark Fisher, *Negro Slave Songs in the United States* (New York: The Citadel Press, 1953), p. 66.

57. Patricia W. Ramero, *I Too Am American: Documents From 1619 to The Present* in International Library of Negro Life and History, 10 vols. (New York: Publishers Company, Incorporated, 1968–69), p. 60.

58. B. A. Botkins, *Lay My Burdens Down: A Folk History of Slavery* (Chicago: University of Chicago Press, 1957), p. 26.

59. Mays, *The Negro's God,* p. 33, citing Richard Allen, *The Life, Experience and Gospel Labors* (Philadelphia: A.M.E. Book Concern), pp. 52–53.

60. Carter G. Woodson, *Negro Orators and their Orations* (New York: Antheneum Publishers, Inc., 1969), pp. 153–154.

61. Lindsay Patterson, *An Introduction to Black Literature from 1746 to the Present* in International Library of Negro Life and History (New York: Publishers Company, Inc., 1968–69), p. 16, citing from *The Interesting Narrative of Olaudah Equiana or Gustavus Vassa, the African* (no page number is given).

62. Mays, *The Negro's God,* p. 109, citing from *Life of Gustavus Vassa, The African* (Boston: Isaac Knapp Publishers, 1837), p. 126.

63. Ibid., p. 116, citing David Walker, *Appeal* (Boston: Revised and Published by David Walker, 1830), pp. 14–15.

64. Bennett, *Before the Mayflower,* p. 156, citing Samuel Ringgold Ward (Bennett does not give a page number, nor is there any indication of the source.)

65. E. Franklin Frazier, *Black Bourgeoisie* (New York: Collier-MacMillan, 1962), p. 163.

66. Mays, *The Negro's God*, pp. 125–126, citing Frederick Douglas, *My Bondage and My Freedom* (New York: Miller, Orton and Mulligan, 1855), p. 215.

67. Alan Lomax and Raqul Abdul, eds., *3000 Years of Black Peotry: An Anthology* (Greenwich, CT: Fawcett Premier Book, 1970), p. 209.

68. Ibid., p. 208.

69. Booker T. Washington, *Up From Slavery* (New York: Airmont Publishing Company, Inc., 1967), p. 136.

70. W. E. B. Du Bois, *The Souls of Black Folk* (Greenwich, CT: Fawcett Publications, Inc., 1961), pp. 43–44.

71. Booker T. Washington, *The Future of the American Negro* (Boston: Small, Maynard and Co., 1907), pp. 53–54.

72. W. E. B. Du Bois, *Dark Water* (New York: Schocken Books, 1969), pp. 3–4.

73. Howard Thurman, "Christ's Message To The Disinherited," *Ebony,* 18 (September, 1963): 60.

74. Ibid., p. 62.

75. Leroy Moore, Jr., "The Spiritual: Soul of Black Religion" *Church History,* 40 (March, 1971): 79.

76. Richard Wright, *12 Million Black Voices* (New York: The Viking Press, 1941), p. 147.

Chapter III

1. Jaroslav Pelikan, *Spirit Versus Structure* (New York: Harper and Row and Publishers, 1968), p. 3 (hereinafter cited as *Spirit Versus Structure*).

2. Roland H. Bainton, *The Age of the Reformation* (New York: D. Van Nostrand Company, Inc., 1956), pp. 99–100 (hereinafter cited as *The Age of the Reformation*).

3. Schweibert, *Luther and His Times*, p. 311, citing Koebler, I.M.R.., p. 387.

4. *Ninety-Five Theses,* 31: 26–33.

5. Bainton, *The Age of the Reformation,* p. 101.

6. Martin Luther, "The Babylonian Captivity of the Church," trans. by A. T. W. Steinhouser and revised by Frederick C. Ahrens and Abdel Ross Wenty,

Vol. XXXVI of *Luther's Works,* ed. Helmut T. Lehmann (Philadelphia: Muhlenberg Press, 1959), 36: 108. (Hereinafter cited as "The Babylonian Captivity of the Church," 36).

7. Ibid., p. 62

8. Ibid.

9. Ibid., p. 116.

10. Ibid., p. 70.

11. Martin Luther, *Concerning the Ministry,* trans. by Conrad Bergendoff, Vol. XL of *Luther's Works,* ed. Helmut T. Lehmann (Philadelphia: Muhlenberg Press, 1958), 40: 35 (hereinafter cited as *Concerning the Ministry,* 40).

12. *Concering the Ministry,* 40: 19.

13. *The Babylonian Captivity of the Church,* 36: 78.

14. Martin Luther, *The Judgment of Martin Luther on Monastic Vows,* trans. by James Atkinson, Vol. XLIV of *Luther's Works,* ed. by Helmut T. Lehmann (Philadelphia: Fortress Press, 1966), 44: 273 (hereinafter cited as *The Judgment of Martin Luther on Monastic Vows,* 44).

15. Gustaf Wingren, "The Concept of Vocation—Its Basis and Its Problems," *Lutheran World,* 15 (1968): 90 (hereinafter cited as Wingren, *The Concept of Vocation*).

16. *The Judgment of Martin Luther on Monastic Vows,* 44:315.

17. Martin Luther, "To the Christian Nobility of the German Nation Concerning the Reform of the Christian Estate," trans. by Charles M. Jacobs and revised by James Atkinson, Vol. XLIV of *Luther's Works,* ed. Helmut T. Lehmann (Philadelphia: Fortress Press, 1966), 44: 141.

18. Ibid., p. 143.

19. Ibid.

20. Ibid., p. 145.

21. Ibid., p. 139.

22. Ibid., p. 172.

23. Ibid., p. 138.

24. Pelikan, *Spirit Versus Structure,* p. 79.

25. "The Babylonian Captivity of the Church," 36: 59.

26. Martin Luther, "Concerning Rebaptism," trans. by Conrade Bergendoff, Vol. XX of *Luther's Works,* ed. Helmut T. Lehmann (Philadelphia: Muhlenberg Press, 1958), 20: 248.

27. Ibid., pp. 248–249.

28. "The Babylonian Captivity of the Church," 36:71.

29. Ibid.

30. Martin Luther, *The Table of Martin Luther,* trans. and ed. by William Hazlitt (London: G. Bell and Sons, Ltd., 1911), p. 20.

31. *Selections From His Writings,* p. 55.

32. Ibid., p. 35.

33. Adolf Harnack, *History of Dogma,* translated from the third German edition of William M. Gilchrist, 7 vols. (Oxford: Williams and Norgate, 1899), 7:216.

34. "The Babylonian Captivity of the Church," 36: 124–125.

35. Ibid., p. 86.

36. Bainton, *Here I Stand.,* p. 53.

37. Crane Brinton, *The Anatomy of Revolution* (New York: Vintage Books, 1965), p. 94.

38. Friedrick Engles, "The Peasant War in Germany," eds. Howard Selsam and others, in *Dynamics of Social Change* (New York: International Publishers, 1970), p. 226.

39. Ibid., p. 216.

40. Kyle C. Sessions, *Reformation and Authority: The Meaning of the Peasant's Revolt* (Lexington, MA: D. C. Heath Company, 1968), p. viii (hereinafter cited as *Reformation and Authority*).

41. Gordon Rupp, *Patterns of Reformation* (London: Epworth Press, 1969), p. 231.

42. Sessions, *Reformation and Authority,* pp. 17–18 citing Friedrick Engles, *The Peasant War in Germany* (New York: International Publishers, 1926, but does not indicate page number).

43. Ibid., p. 18.

44. Ibid.

45. Rupp, *Patterns of Reformation,* citing Gunther Franz, *De decuche Bauernkrieg* (Darmstadt: 1956, but does not indicate page number).

46. Ibid., p. 232.

47. Eldridge Cleaver, *Post Prison Writings,* ed. Robert Scheer (New York: A Ramparts Book, 1969), p. 195.

48. Joseph Lortz, "Reformation and Peasant Rebellion as Phenomena of Change," in Sessions, *Reformation and Authority,* p. 12.

49. Ibid.

50. Rupp, *Patterns of Reformation,* p. 232.

51. Bainton, *Here I Stand,* p. 277.

52. Bainton, *Here I Stand,* pp. 277–278 citing Muntzer, but Bainton does not give the source or the page number.

53. Ralph Z. Moellering, "Attitudes Toward the Use of Force and Violence in Thomas Muntzer, Menno Simons, and Martin Luther," *Concordia Theological Monthly,* 31 (July 1960): 407.

54. Brinton, *Anatomy of Revolution,* p. 108.

55. George Huntston Williams, *The Radical Reformation* (Philadelphia: The Westminister Press, 1962), p. 77.

56. Martin Luther, "Against the Robbing and Murdering Hordes of Peasants," trans. by Charles M. Jacobs and revised by Robert C. Schultz, Vol. XLVI of *Luther's Works,* ed. by Helmut T. Lehmann (Philadelphia: Fortress Press, 1967), 46: 50.

57. Thomas Muntzer, *The Sermon Before The Princes,* trans. by George Huntston Williams, Vol. XXV of *Library of Christian Classics,* editors John Baillie and others (London: SCM Press Ltd., 1957), p. 66.

58. Martin Luther King, Jr., *Stride Toward Freedom* (New York: Perennial Library, 1964), p. 166 (hereinafter cited as *Stride Toward Freedom*).

59. King, *Stride Toward Freedom,* p. 72.

60. Ibid.

61. Ibid.

62. Edward Clayton, *The Peaceful Warrior* (Englewood Cliffs: NJ: Prentice-Hall, 1964), p. 39.

63. King, *Stride Toward Freedom, p. 75.*

64. Ibid.

65. Ibid.

66. *Martin Luther King, Jr. Strength to Love* (New York: Pocket Books, Inc., 1964), p. 168 (hereinafter cited as *Strength to Love*).

67. Ibid., p. 168.

68. King, *Stride Toward Freedom,* p. 75.

69. King, *Strength to Love,* pp. 168–169.

70. King, *Stride Toward Freedom,* p. 78.

71. Ibid.

72. Mahatma K. Gandhi, *Non-Violent Resistance* (New York: Shocken Books, 1961), p. 6.

73. King, *Stride Toward Freedom,* p. 80.

74. Reinhold Niebuhr, *Moral Man and Immoral Society* (New York: Charles Scribner's Sons, 1960), p. 240.

75. King, *Stride Toward Freedom,* p. 80.

76. Ibid., p. 187.

77. L. D. Reddick, *Crusader Without Violence* (New York: Harper and Row, 1959), p. 14.

78. Martin Luther King, Jr., *Where Do We Go From Here: Chaos or Community* (Boston: Beacon Press, 1968), p. 120 (hereinafter cited as *Where Do We Go From Here*).

79. Martin Luther King, Jr., *Why We Can't Wait* (New York: Signet Books, 1964), p. 83 (hereinafter cited as *Why We Can't Wait*).

80. King, *Stride Toward Freedom,* p. 197.

81. King, *Where Do We Go From Here,* p. 193.

82. Ibid., p. 196.

83. Martin Luther King, Jr., "Showdown for Non-Violence," *Look,* 32 (April, 1968): 24 (hereinafter cited as "Showdown for Non-Violence").

84. King, *Why We Can't Wait,* p. 134.

85. Ibid., p. 138.

86. Ibid., pp. 139–140.

87. Ibid., p. 142.

88. King, "Showdown For Nonviolence," p. 25.

89. King, *Where Do We Go From Here,* p. 197.

90. Ibid.

91. Ibid., p. 200.

92. King, "Showdown For Nonviolence," p. 25.

93. Martin Luther King, Jr., "A Testament of Hope," *Playboy Magazine* (January, 1968), p. 8 (hereinafter cited as "A Testament of Hope").

94. *Report of The National Advisory Commission on Civil Disorders* (New York: The New York Times Company, 1968), p. 231.

95. Stokeley Carmichael and Charles V. Hamilton, *Black Power: The Politics of Liberation in America* (New York: Vintage Books, 1967), p. 60.

96. Ibid., p. 80.

97. Niccolo Machiavelli, *The Prince,* translated by Christian E. Detmold (New York: Airmont Publishing Company, Inc., 1965), p. 110.

98. Stokeley Carmichael, "Toward Black Liberation," in *Black and White in America: An Anthology from the Massachusetts Review,* ed. by Jules Chanetzky and Sidney Kaplan (Amherst, MA: The University of Massachusetts Press, 1969), p. 79.

99. Lerone Bennett, Jr., *Confrontation: Black and White* (Baltimore: Penguin Books, Inc., 1966), p. 14 (hereinafter referred to as *Confrontation: Black and White*).

100. Bennett, *Confrontation: Black and White,* p. 236.

101. King, *Why We Can't Wait,* p. 31.

102. Bobby Seale, *Seize The Time: The Story of the Black Panther Party and Huey P. Newton*, ed. Art Goldberg (New York: Vintage Books, 1970), p. 3 (hereinafter cited as *Seize the Time.*)

103. Fanon, *The Wretched of the Earth*, trans. by Constance Farrington (New York: Grove Press, Inc., 1966), p. 46.

104. Seale, *Seize the Time*, p. 31.

105. Ibid., p. 30.

106. Ruth Marion Baruch and Pirkle Jones, *The Vanguard: A Photographic Essay on the Black Panthers* (Boston: Beacon Press, 1970), pp. 44–47.

107. William Shulz, "Intelligence Report on Today's New Revolutionaries," *Readers Digest*, 95 (October, 1969): 122.

108. Gilbert Moore, *A Special Rage* (New York: Harper and Row Publishers, 1971), p. 200 (citing the Black Panther Party newspaper *The Bootlickers Gallery*, but does not give page number).

Chapter IV

1. Henry F. MacKenson, "Historical Interpretation and Luther's Role in the Peasant Revolt," *Concordia Theological Monthly*, 35 (April, 1964): 197–198.

2. Martin Luther, *Psalm 101*, trans. by Alfred von Rohr Sauer, Vol. XIII of *Luther's Works*, ed. by Jaroslav Pelikan (Saint Louis: Concordia Publishing House, 1956). 13: 154–155.

3. Ibid., p. 155.

4. Ibid., p. 159.

5. Erwin Iserloh, "Luther's Christ-Mysticism," in *Catholic Scholars Dialogue With Luther*, ed. Jared Wicks, S. J. (Chicago: Loyola University Press, 1970), p. 39.

6. Thomas M. Lindsay, *A History of The Reformation*, 2 vols. (New York: Charles Scribner's Sons, 1956), 1:316.

7. Martin Luther, *Eight Sermons At Wittenberg 1522*, trans. and ed. by Helmut T. Lehmann, Vol. LI of *Luther's Works* (Philadelphia: Muhlenberg Press, 1959), 51: 77–78.

8. Wingren, "The Concept of Vocation—Its Basis and Its Problems," 15: 87.

9. Claude R. Foster, Jr., "The Wartburg: Symbol of a Synthesis?," *The*

Christian Century, 84 (October, 1967): 1362 (citing Goethe but does not indicate source or page number).

10. John H. Tietjen, The Abiding Validity of the Reformation," in *Accents in Luther's Theology: Essays in Commemoration of the 450th Anniversary of the Reformation*, ed. Heino O. Kadai (St. Louis: Concordia Publishing House, 1967), p. 22.

11. Helmut T. Lehmann, *Introduction to the German Litany and the Latin Liturgy Corrected*, Vol. LIII of *Luther's Works* (Philadelphia: Fortress Press, 1965), p. 149.

12. John Malcus Ellison. *They Sang Through the Crisis* (Valley Forge: The Judson Press, 1961), p. 133.

13. *Selections From His Writings*, p. 73.

14. King, *Strength To Love*, p. 166

15. King, *Why We Can't Wait*, p. 79.

16. King, *Stride Toward Freedom*, p. 84.

17. Ibid., p. 114.

18. Martin Luther King, "I Have A Dream," *Collector's Edition: Martin Luther King Memorial* (April, 1968), p. 23.

19. King, *Why We Can't Wait*, p. 78.

20. Ibid., p. 61.

21. Ibid., p. 87.

22. Ibid., p. 77.

23. Ibid., p. 91.

24. Martin Luther King, Jr., "Then My Living Will Not Be In Vain," *The Ebony Picture Biography* (1968), p. 8.

25. *Selections From His Writings*, pp. 374–375.

26. William L. Shirer, *The Rise and Fall of The Third Reich*, (Greenwich, CT: Fawcett Publications, 1960), pp. 326–327.

27. John Warwick Montgomery, *In Defense of Martin Luther* (Milwaukee: Northwestern Publishing House, 1970), pp. 143–144.

28. John Oliver Killens, *The Black Man's Burden* (New York: Pocket Books, 1969), p. 107.

29. Hans Walton, Jr., *The Political Philosophy of Martin Luther King, Jr.* (Westport, CT: A Negro Universities Press Publication, 1971), p. 114.

30. King, "A Testament of Hope," p. 1.

Chapter V

1. Corretta Scott King. *My Life with Martin Luther King, Jr.*: New York: Avon Books, 1969. P. 285.

2. Resolution from Revised Constitution of the National Baptist Convention, U.S.A., Inc. August 24, 1998.

BIBLIOGRAPHY

Books

Abdul Raqul, and Lomax, Alan, eds. *3000 Years of Black Poetry: An Anthology.* Greenwich, Ct.: Fawcett Premier Book, 1970. 255 pp.

Arndt, William F., and Gingrick, F. Wilbur. *A Greek-English Lexicon of the New Testament and Other Early Christian Literature.* Chicago: University of Chicago Press, 1963. 909 pp.

Augustine. "The Spirit And The Letter." *Library of Christian Classics.* VIII. Edited by John Baillie and others and translated by John Burnaby. Philadelphia: Westminster Press, 1955, pp. 193–250.

Bainton, Roland H. *Here I Stand.* New York: Abingdon, 1951. 422 pp.

———— *The Age of The Reformation.* New York: D. Van Nostrand Company, Inc., 1956. 188 pp.

Baldwin, James. "If They Come In The Morning." *If They Come in the Morning*, Edited by Angela Y. Davis and others. New York: The New American Library, 1971. pp. 19–23.

Baruch, Ruth Marion, and Jones, Pirkle. *The Vanguard: A Photographic Essay on The Black Panthers.* Boston: Beacon Press, 1970. 128 pp.

Bennett, Lerone, Jr. *Before The Mayflower.* Baltimore: Penguin Books, 1968. 435 pp.

———— *Confrontation: Black and White.* Baltimore: Penguin Books, Inc., 1966. 276 pp.

Bonhoeffer, Dietrich. *The Cost of Discipleship.* Translated by Reginald H. Fuller. New York: Macmillan Company, 1963. 285 pp.

Botkins, B. A. *Lay My Burdens Down: A Folk History of Slavery.* Chicago: University of Chicago Press, 1957. 285 pp.

Brinton, Crane. *The Anatomy of Revolution.* New York: Vintage Books, 1965. 310 pp.

Brown, Sterling A., and Davis, Arthur P., eds. *The Negro Caravan.* New York: Arno Press and The New York Times Press, 1970. 1082 pp.

Burton, Ernest DeWitt. *A Critical and Exegetical Commentary on the Epistle to the Galatians.* New York: Charles Scribner's Sons, 1950. 541 pp.

Carmichael, Stokeley, "Toward Black Liberation." *Black and White in America: An Anthology from The Massachusetts Review.* Edited by Jules Chanetzky and Sidney Kaplan. Amherst, Ma.: University of Massachusetts Press, 1969. pp. 76–87.

————, and Hamilton, Charles V. *Black Power: The Politics of Liberation in America.* New York: Vintage Books, 1967. 198 pp.

Cash, W. J. *The Mind of The South.* New York: Alfred A. Knopf, Inc., 1941. 440 pp.

Clayton, Edward. *The Peaceful Warrior.* Englewood Cliffs, N.J.: Prentice-Hall, 1964. 80 pp.

Cleaver, Eldridge. *Post Prison Writings.* Edited by Robert Scheer. New York: A Ramparts Book, 1969. 211 pp.

Cobbs, Price M., and Grier, William H. *Black Rage.* New York: Bantam Books, 1969. 179 pp.

Cochrane, Arthur C. *The Church's Confession Under Hitler.* Philadelphia: Westminster Press, 1962. 317 pp.

Bibliography

Cone, James H. *Black Theology and Black Power.* New York: Seabury Press, 1969. 165 pp.

Conot, Robert. *Rivers of Blood, Years of Darkness.* New York: Bantam Books, 1967. 497 pp.

Douglass, Frederick. *Life and Times of Frederick Douglass,* New York: Collier Books, 1962. 640 pp.

Du Bois, W. E. B. *Dark Water.* New York: Schocken Books, 1969. 276 pp.

———— *The Souls of Black Folk.* Greenwich, Ct.: Fawcett Publications, Inc., 1961. 191 pp.

———— *The World of Africa.* New York: Viking Press, 1947. 276 pp.

Ellison, John Malcus. *They Sang Through The Crisis.* Valley Forge: Judson Press, 1961. 159 pp.

Engels, Frederick. "The Peasants' War in Germany." In *Dynamics of Social Change.* Edited by Howard Selsam and others. New York: International Publishers, 1970. pp. 225–226.

Fanon, Frantz. *The Wretched of the Earth.* Translated by Constance Farrington. New York: Grove Press, 1966. 255 pp.

Fisher, Miles Mark. *Negro Slave Songs in the United States.* New York: Citadel Press, 1953. 223 pp.

Fisher, Paul L., and Lowenstein, Ralph L., eds. *Race and the News Media.* Columbia, Mo: Freedom of Information Center, 1967. 158 pp.

Franklin, John Hope. *From Slavery to Freedom.* New York: Alfred Knopf, 1961. 639 pp.

Frazier, E. Franklin. *Black Bourgeoise.* New York: Collier Books, 1968. 222 pp.

———— *The Negro Church in America.* New York: Schocken Books, 1963. 92 pp.

———— *The Negro Family in the United States.* Chicago: University of Chicago Press, 1966. 372 pp.

Galbraith, John Kenneth. *The Affluent Society.* New York: A Mentor Book, 1958. 286 pp.

Gandhi, Mahatma K. *Non-Violent Resistance.* New York: Shocken Books, 1961. 404 pp.

Grant, Joanne, ed. *Black Protest.* Greenwich, Ct.: A Fawcett Premier Book, 1968. 508 pp.

Harnack, Adolf. *History of Dogma.* Translated by William M. Gilchrist. Vol. VII. London: Williams and Norgate, 1899. 328 pp.

Haselden, Kyle. *The Racial Problem in Christian Perspective.* New York: Harper Torchbooks, 1964. 222 pp.

Herman, Stewart W. *The Rebirth of the German Church.* New York: Harper and Brothers Publishers, 1946. 297 pp.

Herskovits, Melville, Jr. *The American Negro.* Bloomington, In: Indiana University Press, 1964. 92 pp.

Hildreth, Richard. *Despotism in America.* New York: Negro Universities Press, 1968. 307 pp.

Hough, Lynn Harold. *The Meaning of Human Experience.* New York: Abingdon, 1945. 367 pp.

Iserloh, Ervin. "Luther's Chirst—Mysticism." In *Catholic Schools Dialogue with Luther.* Edited by Jared Wicks, S. J. Chicago: Loyola University Press, 1970. pp. 37–58.

Jahn, Janheinz. *Mutu: An Outline of the New African Culture.* New York: Grove Press, 1961. 267 pp.

Johnson, Charles S. *The Shadow of the Plantation.* Chicago: University of Chicago Press, 1934. 215 pp.

Johnson, Clifton H. *God Struck Me Dead.* Philadelphia: Pilgrim Press, 1969. 172 pp.

Bibliography

Johnson, James Weldon, and Johnson, Rosamond J. *The Book of American Negro Spirituals.* New York: Viking Press, 1925. 189 pp.

Jones, LeRoi. *Black Music.* New York: William Morrow and Company, Inc., 1967. 221 pp.

Jones, Major J. *Black Awareness: A Theology of Hope.* New York: Abingdon Press, 1971. 143 pp.

Killens, John Oliver. *The Black Man's Burden.* New York: Pocket Books, 1969. 172 pp.

King, Martin Luther, Jr. *Strength to Love.* New York: Pocket Books, Inc., 1964. 179 pp.

————— *Stride Toward Freedom* New York: Perennial Library, 1964. 209 pp.

————— *Where Do We Go from Here: Chaos or Community.* Boston: Beacon Press, 1968. 209 pp.

————— *Why We Can't Wait.* New York: Signet Books, 1964. 159 pp.

Legum, Colin. *Pan-Africanism: A Short Political Guide.* New York: Frederick H. Praeger, Publishers, 1962. 296 pp.

Lehmann, Helmut T. "Introduction To the German Litany and The Latin Liturgy Corrected." In *Luther's Works.* LIII. Philadelphia: Fortress Press, 1965. pp. 149–150.

Lindsay, Thomas M. *A History of the Reformation* I. New York: Charles Scribner's Sons, 1956. 528 pp.

Luther, Martin. "Against the Robbing and Murdering Hordes of Peasants." *Luther's Works.* XLVI. Edited by Helmut T. Lehmann. Translated by Charles M. Jacobs. Philadelphia: Fortress Press, 1967. pp. 49–55.

————— "The Argument of St. Paul's Epistle to the Galatians." *Luther's Works* XXVI. Edited and translated by Jaroslav Pelikan. Saint Louis: Concordia Publishing House, 1963. pp. 4–12.

———— "The Babylonian Captivity of the Church." *Luther's Works*. XXXVI. Edited by Helmut T. Lehmann. Translated by A. T. W. Steinhauser. Philadelphia: Muhlenberg Press, 1959. pp. 11–126.

———— "Concerning Rebaptism." *Luther's Works*. XL. Edited by Helmut T. Lehmann. Translated by Conrad Bergendoff. Philadelphia: Muhlenberg Press, 1958. pp. 7–44.

———— "Concerning the Ministry." *Luther's Works*. XL. Edited by Helmut T. Lehmann. Translated by Conrad Bergendoff. Philadelphia: Muhlenberg Press, 1958. pp. 7–44.

———— "The Disputations Concerning Justification." *Luther's Works*. XXXIV. Edited by Helmut T. Lehmann. Translated by Lewis W. Spitz. Philadelphia: Muhlenberg Press, 1960. pp. 151–196.

———— "Eight Sermons at Wittenberg, 1522." *Luther's Works*. LI. Edited by Helmut T. Lehmann. Translated by John W. Doberstein. Philadelphia: Muhlenberg Press, 1959. pp. 69–100.

———— "The Eighth Sermon." *Luther's Works*. XXIII. Edited by Jaroslav Pelikan. Saint Louis: Concordia Publishing House, 1959. pp. 56–68.

———— "The Freedom of a Christian." *Martin Luther: Selections From His Writings*. Edited by John Dillenberger. New York: Anchor Books, 1961. pp. 42–85.

———— "The Freedom of a Christian." *Luther's Works*. XXXI. Edited by Helmut T. Lehmann. Translated by W. A. Lambert. Philadelphia: Muhlenberg Press, 1957. pp. 333–377.

————. "The Judgment of Martin Luther on Monastic Vows." *Luther's Works*. XLIV. Edited by Helmut T. Lehmann. Translated by James Atkinson. Philadelphia: Fortress Press, 1966. pp. 251–400.

———— *Lectures on Romans. Library of Christian Classics*. VIII. Edited by John Baillie and others. Translated by Wilheim Pauck. Philadelphia: Westminster Press, 1961. pp. xvii–lxvi.

Bibliography

———— "Luther at the Diet of Worms." *Luther's Works*. XXXII. Edited by Helmut T. Lehmann. Translated by Roger A. Hornsby. Philadelphia: Muhlenberg Press, 1958. pp. 105–131.

———— *Luther's Table Talk*. Edited and translated by William Hazlitt. London: G. Bell and Sons, Ltd. 1911. 390 pp.

———— "Ninety-Five Theses." *Luther's Works*. XXXI. Edited by Helmut T. Lehmann. Translated by C. M. Jacobs. Revised by Harold J. Grimm. Philadelphia: Muhlenberg Press, 1957. pp. 25–33.

———— "Psalm LI." *Luther's Works*. XII. Edited and translated by Jaroslav Pelikan. Saint Louis: Concordia Publishing House, 1959. pp. 303–410.

———— "Psalm 101." *Luther's Works*. XIII. Edited by Jaroslav Pelikan. Translated by Alfred von Rohr Sauer. Saint Louis: Concordia Publishing House, 1956. pp. 145–224.

———— *Sermons of Martin*. Philadelphia: Desilver Thomas and Company, 1835. 204 pp.

———— "Sermon on St. Thomas' Day." *Luther's Works*. II. Edited by Helmut T. Lehmann. Translated by John W. Dobenstein. Philadelphia: Muhlenberg Press, 1959. pp. 17–23.

———— "Theses Concerning Faith and Law." *Luther's Works*. XXXIV. Edited by Helmut T. Lehmann. Translated by Lewis W. Spitz. Philadelphia: Muhlenberg Press, 1960. pp. 109–132.

———— "To George Spenlein." *Luther's Works*. XLVIII. Edited by Helmut T. Lehmann. Translated by Gottfried G. Krodel. Philadelphia: Fortress Press, 1963. pp. 11–14.

———— "To the Christian Nobility of the German Nation Concerning the Reform of the Christian Estate." *Luther's Works*. XLIV. Edited by Helmut T. Lehmann. Translated by Charles M. Jacobs. Philadelphia: Fortress Press, 1966. pp. 123–217.

Machiavelli, Niccalo. *The Prince*. Translated by Christian E. Detmall. New York: Airmont Publishing Company, Inc., 1965. 127 pp.

Mays, Benjamin E. *The Negro's God: As Reflected in His Literature.* New York: Antheneum House, Inc., 1938. 269 pp.

McGiffert, A. C. *Martin Luther: His Life and His Work.* New York: Century Company, 1911. 397 pp.

Meier, August, and Rudwick, Elliott, eds. *The Making of Black America.* New York: Antheneum, 1969. 507 pp.

Mitchell, Henry H. *Black Preaching.* New York: J. B. Lippincott Company, 1970. 248 pp.

Montgomery, John Warwick. *In Defense of Martin Luther.* Milwaukee: Northwestern Publishing House, 1970, 175 pp.

Moore, Gilbert. *A Special Rage.* New York: Harper and Row Publishers, 1971. 276 pp.

Muentzer, Thomas. "The Sermon Before the Princes." *In Spiritual and Anabaptist Writers of Library of Christian Classics* Vol. XXV, edited by George H. Williams. London: SCM Press Ltd., 1957. pp. 49–72.

Murry, Albert. *The Omni-Americans: New Perspectives on Black Experience and American Culture.* New York: Outerbridge and Dienstfrey, 1970. 227 pp.

Myrdal, Gunnar, *An American Dilemma.* Vol. I. New York: McGraw-Hill Book Company, 1964. 520 pp.

Niebuhr, Reinhold. *Moral Man and Immoral Society.* New York: Charles Scribner's Sons, 1960. 284 pp.

Owens, Garfield, Jr. *All God's Chillun: Meditations on Negro Spirituals.* New York: Abingdon, 1971. 144 pp.

Patterson, Lindsay. *An Introduction to Black Literature from 1746 to the Present. International Library of Negro Life and History.* New York: Publishers Company, Inc., 1968. 302 pp.

Pelikan, Jaroslav. *Spirit Versus Structure.* New York: Harper and Row and Publishers, 1968. 149 pp.

Quarles, Benjamin. *The Negro in the Making of America.* New York: Macmillan Company, 1968. 288 pp.

Bibliography

Raushenbush, Walter. *A Theology for the Social Gospel.* New York: Abingdon, 1945. 279 pp.

Report of the National Commission on Civil Disorders. New York: The New York Times Company, 1968. 609 pp.

Riddick, L. D. *Crusader Without Violence.* New York: Harper and Row, 1959. 243 pp.

Roberts, Deotis, Jr. *Liberation and Reconciliation: A Black Theology.* Philadelphia: The Westminster Press, 1971. 205 pp.

Romero, Patricia W. *I Too Am American: Documents from 1619 to the Present. International Library of Negro Life and History.* New York: Publishers Company, Inc., 1968. 307 pp.

Rublowsky, John. *Black Music in America.* New York: Basic Books, Inc., 1971. 150 pp.

Rupp, Gordon. *Patterns of Reformation.* London: Epworth Press, 1969. 427 pp.

Saarnivaara, Uros. *Luther Discovers the Gospel.* Saint Louis: Concordia Publishing House, 1951. 146 pp.

Schwiebert, E. G. *Luther and His Times.* Saint Louis: Concordia Publishing House, 1950. 892 pp.

Seale, Bobby. *Seize the Time: The Story of the Black Party and Huey P. Newton,* edited Art Goldberg. New York: Vintage Books, 1970. 429 pp.

Southern, Eileen. *The Music of Black Americans: A History.* New York: W. W. Norton and Company, Inc., 1971. 552 pp.

Stampp, Kenneth M. *The Peculiar Institution.* New York: Alfred A. Knopf, 1956. 435 pp.

Tennyson, Alfred Lord. "Ulysses." In *Representative Poems.* Edited by Samuel C. Chew. New York: Odyssey Press, 1941. pp. 57–60.

Thoreau, Henry David. "Civil Disobedience, 1849." In *The Portable Thoreau.* Edited by Carl Bode. New York: Viking Press, 1964. pp. 109–137.

Thurman, Howard. *Deep River: Reflections on the Religious Insight of Certain of the Negro Spirituals.* New York: Harper and Brothers, 1955. 93 pp.

Tietjen, John H. "The Abiding Validity of the Reformation." In *Accents in Luther's Theology: Essays in Commemoration of the 450th Anniversary of the Reformation.* Edited by Heino O. Kodai. St. Louis: Concordia Publishing House, 1967. pp. 13–46.

Towsend, Allan W. *A Short Life of Luther.* Philadelphia: Fortress Press, 1967. 75 pp.

Urdany, Lawrence, ed. *The Random House Dictionary of the English Language.* New York: Random House, 1966. 2059 pp.

Walton, Hans, Jr. *The Political Philosophy of Martin Luther King, Jr.* Westport, Ct.: Negro Universities Press, 1971. 137 pp.

Washington, Booker T. *Own Story of His Life and Work.* Naperville, Il: J. L. Nickols and Company, 1916. 510 pp.

—— *The Future of the American Negro.* Boston: Small, Maynard and Company, 1907. 244 pp.

—— *Up From Slavery.* New York: Airmont Publishing Company, Inc., 1967. 192 pp.

Williams, George Huntston. *The Radical Reformation.* Philadelphia: Westminster Press, 1962. 924 pp.

Williams, John H. *The King God Didn't Save: Reflections on the Life and Death of Martin Luther King, Jr.* New York: Pocket Books, 1971. 182 pp.

Woodson, Carter G. *Negro Orators and Their Orations.* New York: Antheneum Publishers, Inc., 1969. 711 pp.

—— *The History of the Negro Church* Washington, D.C.: Associated Publishers, 1945. 322 pp.

—— *The Story of the Negro Retold.* Washington, D.C.: Associated Publishers, 1935. 369 pp.

Bibliography

Wright, Richard. *12 Million Voices*. New York: Viking Press, 1941. 152 pp.

X, Malcolm. *Malcolm X Speaks*. Edited by George Breitman. New York: Grove Press, Inc., 1966. 226 pp.

———— *The Autobiography of Malcolm X*. With the assistance of Alex Haley. New York: Grove Press, 1965. 455 pp.

Periodicals

Bennet, Lerone, Jr. "Liberation." *Ebony* (August, 1970): 36–43.

Foster, Claude R., Jr. "The Wartburg: Symbol of a Synthesis?" *The Christian Century* (October, 1967): 1358–1366.

Franklin, John Hope. "The Bitter Years of Slavery." *Life* (November 22, 1968): 92–120.

Harrington, Michael. "The Will To Abolish Poverty." *Saturday Review* (July, 1968): 10–41.

King, Martin Luther Jr. "A Testament of Hope." *Playboy Magazine* (January, 1968): 1–8.

———— "I Have a Dream." *Collector's Edition: Martin Luther King Memorial* (April, 1968): 18–23.

———— "Showdown for Non-Violence." *Look* (April, 1968): 23–25.

———— "Then My Living Will Not Be In Vain." *The Ebony Picture Biography 1968*, pp. 8–9.

MacKensen, Henry F. "Historical Interpretation and Luther's Role in the Peasant Revolt." *Concordia Theological Monthly* 35 (April, 1964): 197–209.

Moellering, Ralph Z. "Attitudes Toward the Use of Force and Violence in Thomas Muntzer, Menno Simons, and Martin Luther." *Concordia Theological Monthly* 31 (July, 1960): 405–427.

Moore, Leroy, Jr. "The Spiritual: Soul of Black Religion." *Church History* 40 (March, 1971): 79–81.

Muhammad Speaks. "What the Muslims Want" (June 19, 1969): 40.

Shulz, William. "Intelligence Report on Today's New Revolutionaries." *Reader's Digest* (October, 1969): 121–216.

Thurman, Howard. "Christ's Message to the Disinherited." *Ebony* (September 1963): 58–62.

Wingren, Gustaf. "The Concept of Vocation—Its Basis and Its Problems." *Lutheran World* 15 (1968): 87–95.